ESO-SCIENCE WORDBOOK I

ESO-SCIENCE WORDBOOK I

(FOR THE MOORISH HOLY KORAN)

by

BROTHER ERIC MUNGIN BEY D.M.

Copyright © 2018 Eric Mungin Bey

Published by WordVision

All rights reserved. No part of this publication may be reproduced, stored in a retrieval system or transmitted, in any form, or by any means, electronic, mechanical, recorded, photocopied, or otherwise, without the prior written permission of both the copyright owner and the above publisher of this book, except by a reviewer who may quote brief passages in a review.

The scanning, uploading, and distribution of this book via the Internet or via any other means without the permission of the publisher is illegal and punishable by law. Please purchase only authorized electronic editions and do not participate in or encourage electronic piracy of copyrightable materials. Your support of the author's rights is appreciated.

Designed by Vince Pannullo
Printed in the United States of America by RJ Communications.

ISBN: 978-0-9966982-1-4

Contents

An Introduction and Over View 7
The Power of Definition Cover 13
Know Thyself and Allah 17
The Divine Instructions From The Holy Prophet 21

Chapter I: The Creation And Fall Of Man 29
Chapter II: Education of Mary and Elizabeth In Zoan, Egypt 41
Chapter III: Elihu's Lesson-The Unity Of Life 49
Chapter IV: Death and Burial of Elizabeth-Matheno's Lessons-The
     Ministry of Death 55
Chapter V: After The Feast-The Homeward Journey-The Missing
     Jesus-The Search For Him-His Parents Find Him In The
     Temple-He Goes With Them To Nazareth-Symbolic Meaning
     of Carpenter's Tools 61
Chapter VI: Life and Works of Jesus In India Among The Moslems 67
Chapter VII: The Friendship of Jesus and Lamaas-Jesus
     Explains To Lamaas The Meaning of Truth 71
Chapter VIII: Jesus Reveal to The People of Their Sinful Ways 77
Chapter IX: Jesus Attends a Feast In Behar and Here He
     Taught Human Equality 81
Chapter X: Jesus Spake on The Unity of Allah and Man
     To The Hindus 85

This Book 91

AN INTRODUCTION AND OVER VIEW

As the Ancient prophecies predict: "All that has been hidden is being revealed."

All Divine Prophets remedy was to help people in their personal and or national problems. They were to demonstrate (reveal) the Divine Instructions to the wise for their instructions and for the ignorant for their improvement. This was very important to acknowledge this for both for their Salvation. Prophet Noble Drew Ali first published the Holy Koran of The Moorish Holy Temple of Science in the year of 1927. However it was not introduce to the Moors until 1928 at the first Moorish Convention in October. Up until 1929 very little was known within the teachings of the Holy Koran. The Moors did their best for what they had; some interpretation was based on Christian and Masonic teachings. With that understanding the Moors were not elevating to their Potential height which the Prophet intended. Over the course of several years there have been arguments of what was taught and not taught. For one thing that we all should acknowledge is that Prophet Noble Drew Ali stated: "Know Thyself and Allah" to explore that statement we must visit a Moorish historical event in which was written in the book Stolen Legacy by George G.M. James

"In the 8th century A.D. the Moors, i.e., natives of Mauritania in North Africa invaded Spain and took with them, the Egyptian culture which they had preserved. Knowledge in the ancient days was centralized i.e., it belonged to a common parent and system, i.e., the Wisdom Teaching or Mysteries of Egypt, which the Greeks used to call Sophia.

As such, the people of North Africa were the neighbors of the Egyptians, and became the custodians of Egyptian culture, which they spread through considerable portions of Africa, Asia Minor and Europe.

During their occupation of Spain, the Moors displayed with considerable credit, the grandeur of African culture and civilization."

The Prophet gave us our Divine Lesson in chapter 3 verses. 14. "If you would ask me what to study, I would say, yourselves; and you well have studied them; and then would ask me what to study next, I would reply, yourselves."

This school of thought was to teach man to think of the unlimited capacities for progress. The key to Truth is hidden within you. That is why it was said "The Truth shall set you free" Your mind can be a prison or your salvation. In this world you only have two kinds of thoughts one is positive and the other is negative. What brings about any form of education is the ability to think, to learn with its fundamental lessons of words which all have there basic meaning. Words produce many languages and the origin of most languages is most definitely Not Latin, and it is not the origin English, which comes via German and a lot of other influences including (French and Spanish). All worlds' languages may date back a single mother tongue spoken in pre-historic Africa; according to new research humans spoke in a single dialect that proved the catalyst for human civilization. Language was born in Africa, and then the early humans evolved on in this region, and migrated to the rest of the world. In time there were some dramatic changes in human behavior maybe because of the study that they have found suggest that language began to be spread throughout the world and that humans may have actually begun communicating verbally over many years. However or what ever the case may be our cultural minds in Egypt lessons were in stone our visual language of shape, form, color and line to create a message which was called hieroglyphs which had to be reveal by the priest or priestess (Sages). One researcher had said: "Language was our secret weapon, and as soon we got language we became a really dangerous species" You may find this quite true because if a oppressor change another people language those people will begin to change their behavior. Case in point The Bible, which was translated from Hebrew to the English version and this, was given to enslave the people minds, which was through their religion you have witness the result's of this today of the behavior of those who took on that ideology.

A schoolmaster and former Church of England clergyman Robert Cawdrey wrote the first book generally regarded as the English dictionary in 1604. In The United Kingdom Richard Mulcaster often regarded as the founder of English language first published a book called "Elementarie" 1582. Prior to 1864, there were two dictionaries here in United States of American the Dictionary of the English Language (Joseph Worcester) and Webster's Dictionary (Noah Webster) By 1830 began what became known as the "Dictionary War" in brief I will share some light on "The Great Webster's Dictionary Conspiracy" First of all who was Webster, Noah Webster (1757-1843), was a lexicographer (a person who complies dictionaries) and a language reformer which is a type of language planning by massive change to a language. In his lifetime he was also a lawyer, schoolmaster, author newspaper editor an outspoken politician. He went to Yale and graduated in 1778. In 1783, Webster published The American Spelling Book and by 1825 he completed the dictionary, which the first edition was printed in 1828. Webster change the spelling of some words like dawter to daughter – wimmin to women and beleev to believe. This display of words is shown for you to see when the spelling is changed it give a different vibration and meaning. The reason I said this is because if you study Numerology the out come of the hidden meaning of these words will be different. A person who created in such as a spelling book only as you know it is really casting a spell with that said I want you to look up the word Spell in your basic dictionary. Then look up the same word in an online ETYMOLOGY dictionary. Etymology is the study of the origin of words and the ways in which they're meaning have changed throughout history.

Next in the position of Webster's dictionary was Noah Porter the editor of the 1864 Webster's Dictionary. He graduated from Yale in 1931 as a member in the order of the Skull and Bones. After graduation he was a Congregational minister (1836-1846) until becoming a professor of moral philosophy and metaphysics at Yale. He rose to be Yale president in 1871 to 1886. Before I go on with this you may notice that his studies were in moral philosophy and metaphysics. Moral philosophy is the branch of philosophy systematizing, defending, and recommending concepts of right and wrong conduct and Metaphysics, which is a traditional branch of philosophy, that deals with the first principles of things, including, cause, identity, time and space. Now! Hold that thought and remember that he was a Skull & Bone Member. Because of friends in high places gave Webster's dictionaries distinct market placement advantages. By that time Webster's was "America's dictionary" In most cases, a dictionary is merely a compendium (interpretation) of word usage. To be defined in keeping with their common usage words can play a very important lesson in our lives. Stated from his "Moorish Leader's Historical Message To America"

"Read CAREFULLY the doctrines of The M.H.T of S."

Care (n) – serious mental attention - (v) to feel concern or interest

Fully (adj.) entirely, perfectly; completely- containing all that can be received.

I have learned that words have meaning. To discover the hidden meaning in words you must go to the source. To start you must research words by looking into ETYMOLOGY. The Moorish Holy Koran which was given for its Divine Instructions, which were messages through the Prophet's lesson as a continual reminder of the nearness and availability of Allah's instructions. The Prophets work was to receive the Divine message and to deliver that message faithfully. A lesson from the Moorish Holy Koran chapter 23 verse 13; "Teach him Science, and his life shall be useful."

The Divine Prophet's approach their message through Science such as they spoke in PARABLE – A story used to illustrate a moral or spiritual lesson. This was done so that thought which must be developed by the exercise of strength to receive the message through that lesson. As you know the system of education is not what it should be and the ones who created that had disorganize our way of thinking. Thus hope will ever be our beacon light; there is no failure for the human soul, for Allah is leading on and victory is sure. Whatever has been made will be unmade; that which begins must end. This is a process that the mind must go through in order to deciphering (decoding or translating) the cipher (a secret or disguised way of writing a code).

"He hath endued thee with reason, to maintain thy dominion; he hath fitted thee with language, to improve thy society; and exalted thy mind with the powers of meditation, to contemplate and adore His inimitable perfections."

This language is vast as in many ways to see its real hidden words within itself. These teaching of sciences throughout time withheld some of its deepest lessons like Numerology, which is the hidden meaning of numbers and letters. This ties in with sound and vibrations. The Power of Definition was created for the study of SELF-only. All words in this book and symbols are presented to open the mind into self-awareness for your personal salvation. I will define the system that I am using's by revealing a combination of Numerology, Symbolism, Metaphysical and Allegory.

Symbolism – Is the practice or art of using an object or a word to represent an abstract idea. An action, person, place, word, or object can all have a symbolic meaning. Synonyms: emblem, representation, figure, image, sign.

- A figure of speech is often where an object, person, or situation has another meaning other than its literal meaning.
- The actions of character, word, action, or event that have a deeper meaning in context of the whole story

Metaphysical – Referring to an idea, doctrine, or posited reality out side of human sense perception. The philosophy or study that uses broad concepts to help define reality and or understanding of it. Metaphysical studies generally seek to explain inherent or universal elements of reality, which are not easily discovered or experienced in our everyday life. It uses logic based on the meaning of human terms, rather than on a logic tied to human perception of the objective world. Metaphysics might include the study of the nature of the human mind, the definition and meaning of existence, or the nature of space, time, and/or causality (Fate, Karma, Destiny).

Allegory– A story, poem, or picture that can be interpreted to reveal a hidden meaning, typically a moral or political one. Synonyms: metaphor, parable, symbol, emblem.

Color Symbolism – Color is a vital component of many different symbols and many colors have deep symbolism. They are used to depict emotions, personality and feelings and many colors have mystical properties associated with them. The rainbow consists of seven colors. Colors are not what it is but what it gives away.

Their only three major colors (Red Green & Blue). Everything that is physical reflects light; it will have color to your perception. What you reflect will be your color what you hold will not be your color. The color that you reflect will add to your Aura that you carry. Note: Black reflects nothing it holds back everything.

SEVEN THOUGHTS OF WISDOM

- He who knows not and strives to know is a seeker, aid him.
- He who knows not what he should know is a wanderer, guide him.
- He who knows not that he should know is asleep, wake him.
- He who knows not and fears to know is enslaved, free him.
- He who knows not and rejects to know is dead, pass him.
- He who knows not yet claims to know is an impostor, shun him.
- He who knows and shares what he knows is wise, heed him.

THE POWER OF DEFINITION COVER

THE original colors of the Moorish Holy Koran are for a significant reason.

RED is thought to symbolize fire and is associated with power, importance, energy, strength, determination and love. Red is very emotionally intense color. It enhances human metabolism, increases respiration rate, and raises blood pressure. Red also is used to indicate courage. It is a color found in many national flags.

Blue is hope and good health. It is often associated with depth and stability. It symbolizes trust, loyalty, wisdom, confidence, intelligence, faith, truth, and heaven

(State of mind) Blue is considered beneficial to the mind and body. It slows human metabolism and produces a calming effect. Blue is strongly associated with tranquility and calmness. In heraldry, blue is used to symbolize piety and sincerity.

White symbolizes purity, White is associated with light, goodness and innocence. It is the color of perfection and has a positive connotation. White can represent a successful beginning. In heraldry, white depicts faith and purity.

Red, Blue and White that are merge together becomes Purple.

Purple combines the stability of blue and the energy of red. Purple is associated with royalty. It symbolizes power, nobility and ambition. Purple is associated with wisdom, dignity, independence, creativity, mystery, and magic.

Koran – "He read, render" (provide or give, contribute a moral service of what has taken place in the consciousness of man, of the results of his working, either intelligently with the law or unintelligently against it, in seeing his own Salvation). It gives an explanation of Spiritual law as applied to man and women and tells them how to find the kingdom of heaven within. This Spiritual analysis of the Eso-Science Wordbook for the Moorish Holy Koran was prepared for that reason.

Moorish – Meaning the seed from a Divine Essence. And the body signifies as human beings.

Holy Temple of Science – Holy that is whole (complete). Holistic relating to whole: including or involving all of something, especially all of somebody's physical, mental and social condition, not just physical symptoms, in the treatment of illness. Temple, which means to the redeemed mental body. Also a temple is about empowering you. Science is the systematic and orderly arrangement of knowledge, which is the orderly arrangement of truths of Being, does not always conform to intellectual standards, but it is still scientific. This Spiritual science treats of absolute ideas, while mental science treats of limited thoughts. It is an operation of the human Spirit-mind in its endeavor to understanding the how of things.

⑦ the symbol of the Circle represent ought when closed, no beginning and no end; when the four brakes are open it signifies the four dimensions of the mind.

(Intellect, identity, memory and intelligence) The seven indicates the senses of a change after as accomplished cycle and of a positive renewal. It is the sign of the perfect man, and symbol of Divine abundance, it expresses the creation within which the man evolves. Symbol of the infinite numbered, 7 is spiritually, mysticism, wisdom, and success.

In Africa for the Egyptians: it symbolizes a complete cycle, a dynamic perfection. And for the Dogon tribe they consider the number seven as the symbol of the union of opposites, of the resolution of dualism. It is also the mark of the Master of the word. For the Bambaras of Senegal, seven is a symbol of the perfection and the unity.

The indigenous Pueblo of America, the number seven represents the cosmic coordinate of the man.

A Tibetan manuscript has a title "The seven books of Wisdom of the Great Path".

The Buddha would have taken the measure of the universe by making seven steps in each of the four directions.

The man is composed of seven bodies: physics, etheric or vital, emotional or astral, causal, mental, body of divine vitality and the body of divine spirit.

Seven is a mystic number traditionally associated with Venus and more recently with Neptune. It is the number of feelings and of instincts – of the Group Mind, of Love.

Venus – She will represent balance, devotion, desire, creativity and love. Associate with Friday, which is the seven-day of the week. Element is Air

Neptune – Water element. Attributes are intuition, psychic, invention, magic, perception, psychology, philosophy, esotericism, occult, imagination, mysticism, emotion, and shadow/hidden side of life.

Divinely (adj.) c. 1300 "of the nature of the Universal Creator"

Prepared (v.) mid–15c. "Make ready beforehand"

Drew – "Wise" Numerology Soul surge # is 5 this name have a deep inner desire for travel and adventure, and want to set their own pace in life without being governed by tradition.

Ali (Arabic) – "High, elevated" One that have a deep inner desire to use their abilities in leadership, and to have personal independence. They would rather focus on large, important issues, and delegate the details.

Guiding (n.) mid-14c. "One who shows the way"

Allah – "Is the proper name of the Divine Being / Universal Creator"

Great (adj.) 15c. "Of ability, quality, or eminence considerably above the normal or average" Great Spirit (Ojibwa Kitchi Manitou)

Universe (n.) 1580 "The whole world, cosmos, totality of existing things"

Redeem (v.) early 15c. "Deliver from sin and mental death"

Sinful (n.) – "Wrongful thinking that leads to committing an unlawful immoral act"

Fallen stage – "Fallen from a point, a period of life, or step in a process or development which leads one into a mental and moral down fall."

Humanity (n.) late 14c. "Human conduct" or "Human nature, state or quality of being human"

Highest plane – "The Seventh Plane of Existence: Is pure Love, Always super conscious and the Highest Truth"

KNOW THYSELF AND ALLAH

GENEALOGY (n.) early 14c."Generation, descent" " the study of the basic physical unit of heredity along with information within the DNA that provides the coded instructions for the unlearned mind, the passing on of physical or mental which, when translates into, leads to the expression of characteristics genetically from one generation to the another.

Jesus late 12c. It is the Greek form of Joshua. From Late Latin Iesus, From Greek Iesous. Aramaic proper name Jeshua (Hebrew Yeshua, Yoshua). Deliverance through Jehovah.

Life (n.) – "Existence, way of life, perseverance"

Works (n.) late14c. (Someone's) deeds, act, or actions, the things one has done in life," "demonstrations of virtue" The example of his life.

India – (1947) India is a country in South Asia whose name comes from Indus River. The true name 'Bharata' is used as a designation for the country. The land was, therefore, known as Bharatavarsha ('the subcontinent of Bharata') Ancient history: Evidence of the existence and of further discoveries have established fairly clear migration patterns of the people out of Africa. The expression of India suggests an understanding and adoration of that which is of Spirit, law of Being.

Africa – The name Africa, which was originally used by the Romans. However they have changed the spelling, which in turn will change the meaning. The correct name is Afru-ika the true meaning "Mother Land" and this was only in the northwest part of the land and not the whole continent. A Moorish Brother by the name of Al-Hassan ibn Mohammed al Wazzani give the name Afru-ika to that part of the land before the Christian army captured him and they named him Leo Africanus. Hassan was a chronicle writer, traveler, geographer, historian, a diplomat and teacher.

Europe – (522 B.CE) You may find a fiction story behind the origin of this name, nevertheless, here is a short true historical event that was told during the 12th-15th century. A beautiful Moorish Princess named Europa from Morocco was admired for her wisdom and beauty, later on she was kidnaped by a German tribe and brought to their land, which is called Europe today. In later years they name that land after her simply because of the obsession of her radiant of her existence. Therefore Europa was placed on the old maps of the world.

T and O map a symbolized depiction of ancient and medieval world 12c.

Land of Egypt – They called it Egypt because of the Spiritual symbol of the memory -knowledge of knowledge's into the mysteries of faith, and thus from their own power to investigate the truth of Divine arcana (Secrets or mysteries). In ancient times our ancestors had many names the land Kemet (KMT) "black land" because of the fertile black soil and Ta Mery, Ta-Merau or Tameru "The Beloved Land"

With deep appreciation for land our ancestors had a profound Spiritual connection to land, Ancestral law and Spiritually are intertwined with the land, the people and creation, and this forms their culture and sovereignty.

The health of the land and water is central to their culture. Land is their Mother. We live with the land and not living off of it.

NOBLE DREW ALI
THE PROPHET AND FOUNDER OF THE MOORISH
HOLY TEMPLE OF SCIENCE, TO REDEEM THE PEOPLE
FROM THEIR SINFUL WAYS.

THE DIVINE INSTRUCTIONS FROM THE HOLY PROPHET

SULTAN (n.) Arabic 1550s – abstract noun meaning "strength", "authority", "ruler-ship", (Government, Politics, & Diplomacy) the sovereign of a Muslim country, and esp. of the former Ottoman Empire.

Abdul (Arabic) – "Servant of the Universal Creator"

Aziz (Arabic) – "To be powerful or to be cherished, respected, beloved."

Ibn (Arabic) – "son of"

Saud (Arabic) – "Gladness"

Sultan Abdul Aziz Ibn Saud (1880 – 1953) Founder and first King of Saudi Arabia (1932 – 1953). In 1925, Ibn Saud captured holy city of Mecca ending the 700 years of Hashemite rule. On January 8 1926, the leaders of Mecca, Medina and Jeddah proclaimed Ibn Saud King of Hejaz. (Noble Drew Ali was born Jan. 8th 1886). After announcing his Prophet hood in 1925. In that same year The Prophet set up our Moorish Temples and then 1927 the Moorish Holy Koran was published with a picture of Ibn Saud on one side and the Prophet on the other. The Prophet has his right over his heart when you turn the page you will see his hand covering Ibn Saud mouth). This demonstration was to let America know that Noble Drew Ali speaks on the behalf of Islamism.

KNOW THYSELF AND THY FATHER GOD ALLAH

Eighteen – 18 in numerology the sign will be 9 and nine is the symbol of Humanity. It has been called " the goal-setting number." The 1 refers to the self, its accomplishments and feelings. The 8 refer to physical endurance, rhythm and movement. The 9 have a natural instinct toward LAW and it likes law and order. 9 understand Love in its highest sense, it sees only good even in faults.

Year – "Season, any part of a day, hour that which makes a complete cycle.

Events (n.) 1570s "The consequence of anything" (as in the event that); 1580s "that which happens" 1842 Event as "the course of events"

Teaching (n.) c. 1300 "Act of teaching, as that which is taught"

30 – 30 is the conscious power of the cypher (a secret disguised way of revealing a written code, or to put a message into a secret writing; encode. (0) Behind the 3 of self-expression, it represents the completion to achieve a particular aim. And 3 are the numerology number, which is the Creative Principle in the Universal Creator.

Secret Lessons – Pathway of rising into a Higher Level. Secret symbolizes the power of the supernatural (understanding the 7 Universal laws of nature).

Desire (v.) early 13c. "Long for, wish for; demand, expect"

Know (v.) 1590s "To know, perceive, acknowledge, declare"

Teachings (n.) c. 1300 "Act of teaching, "verbal noun from teach (v.) As "that which is taught"

Dear Reader (n.) 1825 – Dear (adj.) early 13c. "Precious, valuable, and beloved" originates: Old Persian "he shall know" - Reader "lectors (someone who reads lessons, scholar"

Falsely use these lessons – Falsely c. 1200 "With intent to deceive, deceitfully" Things may not always be what they seem. Events can often be misinterpreted due to our tendency to attach certain meanings to words base upon egoism (one who is concern for his own interest and welfare) one who furthering ones self interest and that acting against it is immoral. Even at the expense of others these individual's will prey on those who cannot think outside the box (a metaphor that means to think differently, unconventionally-not based on conforming to what is generally done or believed) in other words you must think logic.

Teach (v.) – "To show, point out, declare, demonstrate," also "to give instruction, train, assign, direct; warn"

House in order – House "Temple, literally" "The Universal Creators –house," Family, including ancestors and descendants, especially if Noble c. 1000. The center of civilization. Prophet Noble Drew Ali said: "Honor Thy Father and Thy Mother" that thy days may be long upon the earth land.

Order (n.) early 13c. "Body of persons living under a conscious lessons"

Sake (n.) – "Purpose"

Prophet (n.) Late 12c. "Person who speaks for the Universal Creator; one who foretells, inspired teacher"

Servant (n.) To serve c. 1200 (v.) "Minister, give aid, gives help, to do duty toward, show devotion to"

Worthy (adj.) mid-13c. "Having merit, or a person of merit"

Hire (n.) late 14c. "Appoint"

Reason (n.) c. 1200 "Statement in an argument, statement of explanation or justification" "course; matter; subject; language, speech; thought, opinion,"

"Reckoning, understanding, motive, cause,"

Loosened the keys – revealing of the keys. Three keys are often used to symbolize a like number of secret chambers full of precious objects. They are symbolic re- presentations of initiation and knowledge. The first key, of silver, concerns what psychological understanding can reveal. (This key is Palestine); the second is made of gold, and pertains to philosophical wisdom (This is India); the third and last, diamond confers the power to act. (This key is Egypt). All of these keys have some-thing in common, and it was the relating to the Essenes community and their mystic schools in India, Egypt and Palestine. Origin of their teachings began with Enoch "founder" or "initiator" and then Serapis Bey who was the Chohan "Lord" in Sanskrit of the fourth Ray (The energy of Harmony through conflict) Balance life of the soul and the way of service. Serapis Bey the ascended master who served on Atlantis as a high priest in the Ascension Temple. Before the sinking of Atlantis, he moved the ascension flame to Luxor, Egypt. He established a Temple there and became the Hierarch of the

Ascension Temple. Serapis Bey was the guardian to Earth's evolution from the energy of Venus (Planet of Love) and out from the Ascension school it became the Mystery School. Some names of High Priest are Amenemhat, Amenhotep IV and Manetho.

Many centuries passed in which the Essenes existed as a Mystery School. "Essene"

Denoting "secret" or "mystic" and " "silent" They were well known as the Silent Brotherhood. All Essenes promised to educate their children in the teachings and principles that constituted the foundation of the Essene. They raised each child within the scope of the organization until the child's twelfth year.

Thus we have John the Baptist and Jesus and their parents were of the Essene. As a matter of fact John's father Zacharias was a priest. Very few attained to the highest degree so the Essenes looked forward to the coming of a great Savior who would be born within the fold of their organization and who would be a reincarnation of the greatest of their past leaders their Avatar. So that the teachings can become a highly evolved knowledge to the higher self. Jesus was born in the family of two devout Essenes and in a community of Essenes.

This will ensure that the child will get the very highest education obtainable in any land at that time which had maintained with their other branches in foreign lands such as the Supreme Temple in distant Egypt and minor temples in Palestine, India and other places. This will ensure to teach him to be the "Son of God" and not as we were told that he is the Son of God. Other notables that were involved with the Essenes were Elijah and Philo. This has been held in secrecy for many centuries.

Authority (n.) early 13c. "Inspired by Spirit within. The Spirit of Truth is the one and only authority in the study of Truth.

Pamphlet (n.) 12c. A guide (guidance) about love

Industrious (adj.) – "Characterized by energy, effort, and attention"

Industry (n.) late 15c. "Cleverness, skill," "diligence, activity, zeal," "to build" "Trade or manufacture"

Acts (n.) late 14c. "A thing done." also "To do, set in motion, to lead, guide."

Moabites – "Of or belonging to Moab" Thoughts springing from and belonging to that in consciousness which Moab signifies.

Hamathites - "Of or belonging to Ham" A descendant of Canaan the son of Ham.

A thought or tendency in man that belongs to the body consciousness (Canaan), or to the Hamath consciousness (confidence in the quality or character of being material or composed of matter and its results)

Canaanites – The elemental life forces in the subconsciousness. Under sense thought and expression they are that the meaning of Canaanite.

Land of Canaan – The Land of Canaan represents the unlimited elemental forces of being in which man is placed and to which he gives character through faith in Allah as omnipresent Spirit. The land of Canaan represents humbleness and receptivity.

Joshua (Heb.) – Jehovah is salvation; Jah is savior; Jehovah is deliverer; whom Jehovah makes triumphant; Jehovah is the victory.

Pharaoh's - "Title for Kings" Pharaoh means the sun. He is ruler of the solar plexus, the sun center in the subconscious mind. By being ruler of Egypt means that he rules the mystery or secret of man.

Kingdoms – (1690) "In order to find this kingdom, man must become conscious of Divine Mind and its realm of divine ideas, and be willing to adjust his/hers thoughts to divine standard"

Morocco – Morocco is an ancient country with a strong sense of culture. The English name "Morocco" originates from Spanish name "Marruecos". This, in turn, derived from "Marrakesh". Marrakesh remains the current name for Morocco in many South Asian language's such as Persian (Iran), Urdu (Pakistan), Punjabi (India) and Pashto (Afghanistan). Also in Egyptian and Middle Eastern Arabic literature the name for Morocco (as a distinct country/state) was "Marrakesh", until about the 2nd half of the 20th century. In Turkish, Morocco is still known as "Fes", a name derived from its ancient capital city Fes.

The word "Marrakesh" is made of the Moabite word combination Mur N Akush

Meaning, "Land of the Creator". The recorded history of Morocco begins with the Phoenician (Canaanites) colonization of the Moroccan coast between the 8th and 6th centuries BC. Although the area was inhabited by the Moabites for some two thousand years before that. Morocco was at its most powerful under a series of Moorish dynasties, which rose to power south of the Atlas Mountains and expanded their rule northward.

Algiers – "The Island" Ancient Algeria was the site of the highest state development of Middle stone age Flake tool techniques. Prehistory of Central North Africa: Early inhabitants of the central Maghrib (also seen as Maghreb; designates North Africa west of Egypt) North Africa During the Classical Period: Phoenician (Canaanites) traders arrived on the North African coast around 900 B.C. and established Carthage (in present day Tunisia) around 800 B.C. During the classical Period, Moabite civilization was already at a stage in which agriculture, manufacturing, trade, and political organization supported several states.

Algiers became the center of the Ottoman authority in the Maghreb. Dey was the title given to the rulers of the Regency of Algeria and Tripoli from under the Ottoman Empire from 1671 onwards.

Tunis – Tunis derives from the Phoenician (Canaanites) goddess "Tanith" She was equivalent to the moon-goddess Astarte. Carthage was founded in the 9th century B.C. on the Coast of North Africa, in what is now Tunisia. It developed into a significant trading empire throughout the Mediterranean, and was seen as home to a wealthy and brilliant civilization.

The city stated as one of a number of Phoenician (Canaanites) settlements in the western Mediterranean that were created to facilitate trade from the city of Tyre on the coast of what is now Lebanon. Most Phoenician (Canaanites) cities had fewer than 1,000 inhabitants, but Carthage and few other cities developed into large, self-sustaining, independent cities. Ancient sources concur that Carthage had become perhaps the wealthiest city in the world via its trade and commerce. According to tradition, Queen Dido in some sources she is also known as Eilissa founded the city.

Tripoli - "Three cities" Tripoli was founded in the 7th century B.C. by the Phoenician (Canaanites), who named it Oea. Oea and surrounding Tripolitania was prosperous, and reached a golden age in the 2nd and 3rd centuries AD. Around the beginning of the 3rd century AD, it became known as the Regio Tripolitania, meaning "region of the three cities", namely Oea (modern Tripoli of Libya).

European maritime powers paid the tribute (payment made periodically by one state or ruler to another, especially as a sign of impendence) exacted by the rulers of the privateering states of North Africa (Algiers, Tunis, Tripoli [today Libya}, and Morocco) The Europeans name the area Barbary Coast.

ETC – Earth, Territory and Country

End Notes:

In regard's to the word Pamphlet which signifies a moral tone, and in the spiritual direction of its contents, such a tone and spiritual meaning as we should find in the life and events of Yeshua (Jesus) Study the life the expression of being which manifest as energy, activity, and force. Life is the acting principle; substance is the thing acted upon. The idea behind the stories of his life is that you must conceive a relevant analogy to your own situation.

Keys – Means Knowledge, in which a problem will be solved and you will be opening the door to opportunity.

CHAPTER I

THE CREATION AND FALL OF MAN

FALL of man – Man's failure to recognize his/hers divinity by the ignorance of not knowing his relation towards the Universal Creator. By this error he/she falls deeply into a state of lowering in status, quality and character in thought.

Creation (n.) late 14c."The order of creation is from the formless to the formed, from the invisible to the visible". This goes on continuously, and there is never a beginning or an ending to the process. Creation is the original plan of an idea in Spirit.

Fall (n.) c. 1200 "A descent from a higher to lower position (as by gravity).

Fall (v.) 1751 "take place or position"

Time (n.) - "Limited space of time"

Man (n.) - "In the general language Man in reference represents person (male or female) Human being"

Thoughts of Allah – "The moving force of Energies sent out by the Universal Creator"

Circumscribed (v.) late 14c."Limit, restrain, confine, set the boundaries of."

Finite (adj.) early 15c."Limited in space or time, finite", "to limit, set bounds; come to an end"

Infinite (adj.) late 14c."Eternal, limitless, endless, and boundless"

Mind (n.) late 12c. The mind is a tool for exploration, not for drawing conclusions and only a thought process. Caution a prejudice mind cannot receive or reveal the reality of life. "The mind is the seat of perception of five the senses." 4 dimensions of the mind are (Intellect, identity, memory and intelligence)

Comprehend (v.) mid 14c. "To understand, to perceive, to seize or take in the mind"

Change (n.) c. 1200 "Act or fact of changing, Meaning" "a different situation" is from 1680s.

Change (v.) early 13c. "To substitute one for another; to make (something) other than what it was" (transitive): from late 13c. As "to become different" "to change, alter; exchange, switch.

Cease (v.) c. 1300 "To come to an end, stop, cease; give up, desist" also "The fact or process of ending or brought to an end" "go away, withdraw, yield"

Souls of men - Thinking, understanding, reasoning, wiling, call not these the Soul. They are the its actions, but they are not its essence. It's Higher than all is the object of thy senses. The senses were ordained to bring into the mind mere pictures of the things that pass away; they do not deal with real things; they do not comprehend eternal law. It is used for the spiritual and emotional part of a person, animate; life, living being.

Spirit (n.) mid-13c. "Animating or vital principle in man, breath"

"Ones life force of existence of their very being"

Creative Fate – Creative 1670s, "having the quality of creating" Fate late 14c "Is the development of events beyond a person's control regarded as determined by a supernatural power" The Seven Creative Spirits Elohim, who in their boundless power, created everything that is, or was. Study chapter 11 from the Moorish Holy Koran.

Spirit Man –Your spirit is the highest aspect of who and what you are. It is the direct fragment of the Divine Life of the Universal Creator. This body vibrates at the highest frequency. The Spirit is the highest expression of universal individuality which contains, within, many keys to truth and has its roots with Allah and with all the spirits, within the highest realm of Creation; a realm, which we cannot even begin to comprehend, here on the Earth plane.

Plane of Soul – The plane of soul exist in the realm of pure spirit, beyond duality.

The soul body holds the essence of your spirit that will function on the plane of soul.

Function (n.) 1530s "One's proper work or purpose; power of acting in a specific proper way"

Physical Plane – Plane of things that are made manifest. This plane is the densest of the seven planes; where we presently reside.

Hear (v.) 1680 "To call attention"

Cherubim – late 14c. This name is a title "Angel who serve as heavenly counselor"

"The guardians of light, and stars. Remote from your plane of reality, still their light touches your lives, the divine light that filter down from the first Sphere"

Cherubim are the bearer for the faithful, the Angel of protection of sacred life. The inner spiritual life protected from outer, coarser consciousness.

Seraphim – 1667 this name is a title "Angel who serve as heavenly counselor" The highest order of highest hierarchy Seraphim and Cherubim, the celestial beings. These angels are considered to be the light-burners, and will be watchful over the true heart and faith. They provide fuel on our spiritual path.

Protoplast (n.) "A person or thing that is formed first; original"

Earth (n.) c. 1400 "Represent the idea with manifestations in the earth to correspond"

Plant (n.) 1630 "The signification of a plant, is to regenerate, for regeneration, similar is the case with regeneration in man" It is said regeneration continually, because regeneration begins in man, but never ceases, being continually perfected, not only while he lives in the world, but also in the other life to eternity; and yet it can never arrive at any such perfection that it can be compared to the Divine.

Beast (n.) c. 1200 "Beast signifies man's affections evil affections with the evil, and good affections with the good"

Creeping things of the earth – "Creeping things are symbolic of the animal desires and instincts that have evolved with us and creep within the lower nature of man"

Fish that swim – "The symbolic nature of Fish and water is that the two are connected in life" Water symbolizes the depths of the unconscious, and the fish are the "live material from the depths of the personality, relating to fertility and the life giving powers of the maternal realms within us" Fish can also be symbolic of faithful submerged in the waters of life.

Birds that fly – "Birds symbolize the power that helps people to speak reflectively and leads them to think out many things in advance before they take action" "They also represent the human desire to escape gravity, to reach the level of angel.

Winds that blows – "It is the messenger of the divine intervention, and it is the vital breath of the universe" Wind often represents the fleeting and transient, the elusive and the intangible. "Breath in speaking"

Thunders and lightning's – "Thunder is typically perceived as an expression of the sentiments of the Universal Creator, it is considered a vehicle for conveying divine wrath. While Thunder is a voice, a lighting bolt is a weapon" The bolt of lightning is a traditional symbol of sudden illumination and the destruction of ignorance.

Sky (n.) c. 1200 "The sky represents infinity, eternity, immortality, and transcendence" The sky is symbolic of order in the universe.

> Spirits of the fire – Positive qualities: transformation, zeal, creation, destruction, decisiveness, power of creativity, and daring, active life force.
> South – Vowel I / Planet: Mars – Represents form. (Physical energy)
> Energy: Masculine, projective
> Magical Power: To will
> Chakra(s): Solar Plexus
>
> Spirits of Water - Positive qualities: Understanding, emotional,

psychic, devotion, mercy, subconscious, purification, compassion, and meditativeness.

West - Vowel O / Planet: Venus – Represents taste. (Healing)
Energy: Feminine, receptive
Magical Power: To Dare
Chakra(s): Navel, (Heart)

Spirits of Earth: Positive qualities: Consistency, conscientiousness, perseverance, abundance, solid foundation, responsibility, carefulness, firmness, reliability, ambition, respectfulness, fertility and nurturing.

North - Vowel U / Planet: Mercury – Represents smell. (Communication)
Energy: Feminine, receptive
Magical Power: To be Silent
Chakra(s): Root (base of spine)

Spirits of Air - Positive qualities: Vigilance, care-freedom, kind hearted, trusting nature, clarity, new life, power of the mind, communication, diligence, and joy.

East – Vowel E / Planet: Saturn– Represents touch. (Transforming)
Energy: Masculine, projective
Magical Power: To know
Chakra(s): (Throat, 1st Eye)

Wisdom speaks – Intuitive knowing; spiritual intuition; the voice of Allah within as the source of our understanding; mental action based on the Love Truth within. Wisdom includes capacity for making decisions, the making of distinctions, intuition, and all the departments of mind that come under the head of knowing. This "knowing" capacity transcends intellectual knowledge. Spiritual discernment always places wisdom above the other faculties of the mind and reveals that knowledge and intelligence are auxiliary to understanding.

Highest plane of spirit life – "Unexplainable to anyone on the lower plane"

Measure (n.) c. 1300 "Limit, boundary, quantity, dimension; occasion, time"

Concern (v.) early 15c. "Perceive, distinguish," "also "refer to, relate to,"

Everlasting - early 13c. "Eternal" "eternally" "eternity" "to endure forever"

Seed – late 14c. The creative idea inherent in the word. Its nature is inherited from its parent source, Allah. The seed is a generative center through which intelligence manipulates substance and produces form. In itself it is powerless to produce anything, but it is the avenue through which interior forces manifest in the outer. Women and Man draws on the universal forces within and without, just as the trees draw on the invisible Spirit and earth, air, and water.

Potencies (adj.) early 15c. "Be powerful, able, capable"
Attributes (n.) late 14c. "Qualities belonging to someone or something"
Perfect (adj.) early 15c. "Finished, completed, ready"
Source (v.) "Obtain from a specified source, Meaning "a first cause"
Unfold (v.) "To disclose, reveal"
Especial Plant – Especial "Pre-eminent, important qualities" Planets represent an image of life, expressive of the manifestation of the cosmos and of the birth of forms. Another aspect of plant-symbolism is the annual cycle, in consequence of which they sometimes symbolize the mystery of death and resurrection.

Deeply (adj.) - via sense development. "Profound, mysterious, deepness, depth"

Unfold to show the Flower – Unfold "to disclose, reveal" The Flower and the blossom are both universal symbols of young life. Each flower has a separate meaning characterized by the flower in its essence, and the flower in its shape.

Manifest (adj.) late 14c. "Clearly revealed"
Soil (n.) c. 1300 "Soil of the Soul"

Bud (n.) late 14c. "To be in a undeveloped stage or condition"

Heart – 1500 "The soul"

Lord (n.) mid-13c. "The activity of spiritual I AM as the ruling consciousness, the spiritual man our divine consciousness; the creative power within us" As Lord consciousness is one dominion. When we enter into our lordship we rule. We rule over ourselves, our thoughts, our body, our environment, and all the creatures and creations of the earth.

Husbandman – "The masculine principle" also "a gardener; of the people"

Apace (adj.) mid-14c. "At a pace, rate of motion"

Kingdom of the soul – The king of the soul is comprised of those many living souls who have completed the journey Home and who have their real residence on those higher levels of consciousness towards which we are moving.

Hark (v.) late 12c. "Listen"

Creature (n.) late 13c. "Anything created," also "living being"

Ether (n.) late 14c. "The spiritual substance in which we live, move and being governed and sustained by ideas, and ideas have no physical dimension" Also known as the fifth element, which is Ether. A represents the symbol. Spirit, which is Also known as the 5th element that signifies infinity and pure energy.

Vibrate (v.) 1610s "Move quickly to and fro;" Set in tremulous motion.

Rhythm (n.) 1550s "Metrical movement," or "movement in time, measured flow movement, rhythm in arrangement, order; form, shape, wise, manner; soul, disposition" Rhythm from which all motion comes.

Essence of life – The substance in which all things exist and out which all things are made.

Perfumes and the odors – Perfumes is feminine (pre- is a prefix which means before, prior to, early and in front of). Fume meaning smoke while perfume literally means through the sweet smoke. Odor points to a sense of the powerful spiritual reality that fragrance of new life points back to the world we came from. This was the scent of its own essence or the divine fragrance of the Female Spirit. Also scent or perfume in its association with the general symbolism of the air is equivalent to the wakes or tracks that mark the passage of solid bodies through the atmosphere, and consequently symbolic of memories or recollections.

Sensation (n.) "A state of excited interest or feeling derived from stimulation of the sense organs" Spirituality, lifts up this divine creation and restores it to its original beauty. Through cultivation of the spiritual nature, sensation crowned with purity. A physical feeling or perception resulting from something that happens to or comes into contact with the body.

A body beautiful - The body beautiful is something no one can describe and yet everyone is able to see it. These are typical characteristics of a spiritual subject: it is impossible to describe what spirit is unless and until you have felt it. But once you have felt the beauty of your spirit, you will see it everywhere.

Tarries (v.) "Stay longer than intended; delay leaving a place"

Garb (n.) c. 1600 "Person's outward appearance"

The perfumes and odors and the true sensations and all of Love were clothed in flesh – First Female /feminine and man was clothed in flesh. – Then Man/masculine.

One of the Seven Universal Laws. Generation (Gender) everything has its masculine and feminine principles. Within our own individual spheres of existence we know that every male has elements of feminine energy, and every female carries the components of the masculine.

Clothed with flesh – "Clothed is in reference to characteristic" and Flesh at times is used interchangeably with "soul and body", and credited with the emotions and responses of the whole person. If at times the outer being (flesh) is distinguished from the inner (heart/soul).

Pass through all the ways of life – Pass (v.) late 13c. "to move forward, make one's way" "to go through an examination successfully"

Carnal (adj.) c.1400 "Physical, human, mortal"

Foe (n.) 1600 "Adversary, enemy or opponent"

Nature that spring forth - Nature (n.) late 13c. "Restorative powers of the body, bodily processes; powers of growth" Course of things form birth.

Eso-Science Wordbook I

Thought must be developed by the exercise – The act of training the mind to think of Allah's attributes as forces that are being incorporated into the mind as one incorporates strength into the body.

Exercise (v.) late 14c. "The act of training the mind to think of the Universal Creator's attributes as forces that are being incorporated into the mind as one incorporated strength into the body, This is demonstrated by Prayer, meditation, and fasting from untrue ideas"

Strength (n.) "The energy of Allah, Freedom from weakness; stability of character; power to withstand temptation; capacity to accomplish. Strength is physical, mental, and spiritual" All strength originates in Spirit, thought and the word spiritually expressed being the manifestation.

Birthrights (n.) 1530s "That is which one is entitled by reason of birth, by the process of creation all of humanity is considered children of Allah and blessed with a posterity perpetuated through the ongoing natural birth process. All that is given to you at birth such as a soul and body is unlike anything else in this world. Our capabilities are exceptional within the power of the thought" By birth (inheritance) the extreme high value of your legal & spiritual right.

Gratify (v.) 1530s "To show gratitude to, to do favor to, oblige, pleasing"

Regain (v.) 1540s "Reclaim, re-conquer, recover, retrieve"

Lost Estate – "One who is unable to find ones way from a period or human condition of life"

Heritage (n.) c.1200 "That which may be Spiritual inherited"

Conflict (n.) mid- 15c."Meaning struggle"

Suffer (v.) mid-13c. "Undergo experience to subjected to, receive, endure, adversity, anguish, misery, stress, grief and trauma"

Trial (n.) mid-15c."Act or process of a testing, a putting to proof by examination"

Temptation (n.) "An experience or state of being tempted"

Manifold (adv.) "In various ways, numerous, abundant"

Rule (v.) c. 1200 "To control, guide, direct"

Rule (n.) c. 1200 "Principle or maxim governing conduct, formula to which conduct must be conformed"

Station (n.) late 13c. "A place were a specified activity or service is based"

Station (v.) "Put in or assign to a specified place for a particular purpose"

Sun – "The star around which earth orbits" also signifies the realm of consciousness that has been illumined by Spirit.

Solar stars - Solar System "The collection of eight planets and their moons on orbit around the Sun"

Protector (n.) mid-14c. "Shelter, defense; guardianship, that which protects"

Guide (n.) mid-14c. "One who shows the way"

Guide (v.) mid-14c. "To lead, direct, conduct" guide, leader.

Lead (v.) - "Guide" Bring forth.

Victory (n.) - "Conqueror"

Redeem (v.) - "Compensate for the faults or bad aspects of (something)" Save

Purpose (n.) c. 1300 "Intention, aim, goal"

Fall (v.) - "Fail"

Untrammeled (adj.) 1530s "Not deprived of freedom of action or expression; not restricted or hampered"

Complete (adj.) - "To fill, to fulfill, to finish (a task)."

Overcome (v.) - "To reach, overtake," also "to conquer, prevail over"

Yea (adj.) - "So, yes"

Thus (adv.) - "In this way, as follows"

Hope (v.) - "Wish, expect, look forward (to something)"

Beacon light – As a source of light or a sign serving as a signal or guide, Beacon take on the symbolism of illuminating the way to spiritual enlightenment and to sanctuary for the Spirit.

Failure (n.) 1640s, Act of failing, "Be lacking; not succeed"

Die (v.) mid-12c. "To die, pass away, "become senseless"

Conquer (v.) - "One who attains mastery over sense consciousness" defeat, vanquish, win, and conquer.

Open out – "To disclose, reveal" also become manifest, to open to or exposed to"

Holy Breath – Divine Feminine Energy

Serve (v.) late 12c. "To render, habitual obedience to, "also minster, give aid"

Attain (v.) c. 1300 "To succeed in reaching"

Blessedness - "To consecrate, make holy, give thanks. Meaning "gift from Allah"

End Notes

The following chapters are in connection with chapter one.

Chapters - 3 – 7 – 8 – 11 – 35 – 36 -38

The Fall of man – Are those who fail to recognize the Spirit-mind shining within them and they dwell in a continuous in a state of darkness and ignorance. In general sense the fall represents the descent of Spirit into matter.

East also means a deeper dimension of intelligence within us.

Sacred vowels are pathways within a word, which gives it life that comes from their element. It leads us to the inner power of that word. They are symbols that have its own meaningful way towards connecting that meaning with our thoughts so that we may comprehend their inner meaning.

Five senses (intelligence)

<u>Outward</u>	<u>Inward</u>
Sight:	Perception
Taste:	Judgment
Smell:	Perceive (notice or recognize)
Touch:	Examine
Hear:	Attention

CHAPTER II

EDUCATION OF MARY AND ELIZABETH IN ZOAN, EGYPT

EDUCATION (n.) 1530's True education is when you learn about self, moral and spiritual concepts that pupils need to learn are what human beings experiencing and to drew forth from within, through meditation. To Know Thyself and the deep truths of Allah. The human mind must investigate the origin, nature, methods, and limits of knowledge. Consider your "true" self, that is, who you really know yourself to be. Then, ask yourself where did human knowledge come from? What does it mean and what is the process by which this became known? Education provides the clearest insight into what the thinking mind actually inquires into. The focus here is not what you know, but how we know that we know that.

Herod (Gk.) - "Son of a hero" The king of Judea. He signifies the ruling will of the physical, the ego in the sense consciousness. This ruling ego is temporal because it does not understand man's true origin or law of man's being. It is narrow, jealous, and destructive. Under its rule man does not fulfill the law of his being, and another ego must supplant the ego of sense. Herod implies as ruler of the lower nature.

Archelaus (Gk.) - "The prince of the people" Ruler of the people, son of Herod. A phase of the sense will, or ruling power in sense consciousness.

Jerusalem (Heb.) - Jerusalem was established as a Canaanite city, Meaning habitation of peace; dwelling place of peace; foundation of peace; constitution of harmony; vision of peace; abode of prosperity.

Jerusalem signifies that in man it is the abiding consciousness of spiritual peace, which is the result of continuous realization of spiritual power tempered with spiritual poise and confidence.

Honor (n.) c. 1200 "Glory"

Council (n.) early 12c. "Assembly; council meeting; body of counselors"

Claimant (n.) 1747 "Claim"

Throne (n.) c. 1200 "Symbol of royal power"

John (Heb.) - Jehovah bestows mercifully; Jah is gracious. He signifies a high intellectual perception of Truth, but one not yet quickened of Spirit. John represents that attitude of mind in which we are zealous for the rule of Spirit. This attitude is not spiritual, but a perception of spiritual possibilities and an activity in making conditions in which Spirit may rule.

Jesus in (Aramaic) - "Signifies The I in man, the self, the directive power, raised to divine understanding and power" The I AM identity.

Joseph (Heb.) - "One who adds; increasing in faithfulness" Joseph signifies the state of consciousness in which we increase in character along all lines; we not only grow into a broader understanding but there is an increase of vitality and substance. Joseph name came from Jeshua, Yeshua, or Yoshua

Joseph in Egypt symbolizes the word of the imagination in subconsciousness, or the involution of high spiritual idea. He also represents our highest perception of Truth, dealing with the realm of forms and bringing it into a more orderly state.

Mary –Mery/Meryt (Egyptian) Meaning "Cherished" or "beloved"

Miyam (Heb.) - Meaning "The living fragrance from the sea of life" The wife of Joseph and mother of Yeshua (Jesus) She signifies the divine motherhood of love. The feminine, the soul, the affection and emotional phase of man's being, both when seemingly bound and limited by sensate thought, and in its freed, exalted state.

Zoan – "Motion" Old Egypt, "Strong hold" a city on the Tanitic branch of the Nile, called by the Greeks Tanis.

Elihu (Heb.) - "My Jehovah is He" The name Elihu also signifies the recognition by man that his true inner self is Spirit. Brother Elihu was a teacher in Zoan Egypt.

Salome (Heb.) - "Peace" She represents the soul clothed in the thought of wholeness, soundness, love, peace, and truth. Sister Salome was a teacher in Zoan Egypt.

Elizabeth – Elisheba (Heb.) - Meaning, "Allah is my Oath " Elizabeth was the wife of Zacharias the priest, mother of John. She represents the soul in the feminine or love consciousness.

Hast (v.) early 13c. "Urgency"

Marveling (v.) c. 1300 "To be filled with wonder, to wonder at, be astonished"

Deliverance (n.) c. 1300 "Action of setting free" in physical or spiritual senses"

No happenings: law governs all events – One of the Seven Universal Laws. The (Cause and Effects) states, "Every cause has a effect; every effect has a cause" Nothing happens by chance or outside the Universal Laws. For every action there is an equal and opposite reaction. Every human thought, word and deed is Cause that sets off a wave of energy throughout the universe, which in turns creates the effect whether desirable or undesirable. The law states the effect must to physical manifestation. This is why good thoughts, words, emotions, and deeds are essential for a better world for the all create good effects.

Olden Times – Ancient Times

Ordain (adj.) late 13 "To appoint or admit to the ministry of" "place in order, arrange, prepare; consecrate, designate" Sense of "to set (something) that will continue in a certain order" is from early 14c.

Sacred School of Thought – The Ascension Temple was the origin of many schools of thought. Some are called today as the Mystery School. In the study of ancient mystery schools, were the teaching of spiritual wisdom, esoteric knowledge. Esoteric meaning "Intended for or likely to be understand by only a small number of people with a special knowledge of interest" These schools existed from Lemuria (The continent of Mu) and Atlantis to Egypt, Australian aborigines and Greece. The ancient schools of the Essenes teach us about the true meaning of prayer. The study of the Hopi, Navaho and Quechua of Peru not only engages us in shamanism but in our celestial connection. A seeker on the path of self-mastery is a goal of an Adept, which is to know, to experience and to reveal.

Sacred Grove – A small forest or woodland area that are connected to the feminine forces within the universe. They can give you insight into your life circumstances and lessons. These sacred groves stir within us our own creative energies so that we can apply them to our life. They enable us to face our fears and awaken the unconscious mind so that we can employ it in our conscious activities.

Esteem (n.) mid- 14c. "Account, value, worth," Meaning "high regard" is from 1610s.

Thrice (adj.) - "Three" Three denotes divine perfections, Wisdom, Will, and Love.

Chosen (n.) 1200 "Elect, select," especially those selected by The Universal Creator.

Promise (n.) c. 1400 "A pledge, and vow"

Solid Rock – Rock is the ultimate embodiment permanence, stability and reliability. This suggests that you will find a smooth path through your life.

Foundation Stone – "The lessons of redeeming ourselves from bondage to sense, to be sustained by the inner or spiritual food (hidden gift) which is understanding of Truth and which is the foundation upon which will build up and develop our true self"

Temple of the Perfect Man – Perfect man is the manifestation of the Higher-self the Temple within. This attainment requires careful training of thoughts. One must pass through all the trials, temptations, and mental variations of each of us, "yet without sin," that is, not falling under the dominion of negative thoughts. When we rise above the demands of the flesh-and sense world he/she will reach the divine nature, which is permanent, and that is the Temple that shall never be destroyed.

Measure Time by Cycle Ages – Cycle Age are our Life Cycle or Law of Cycle. When we are born, we human beings have our cycles. The earth revolves around the Sun every 365 days and this results in rhythm. When we are born we came on earth with our individual rhythm and so we vibrate on this frequency. The day that we arrive here starts from that day on for 52 days, which began your first cycle. The next 52 days will be your second cycle and so on. Each 52 days completes one cycle. This is done by 7 times. 7X52= 364. Within the 52 days you have a life cycle, business cycle and a health cycle.

Gate to every age – This is Astrology. Example Aquarian Age, Piscean Age

Deem (v.) - "Regard, or consider in a specified way" also "View, think"

Milestone (n.) 1746 "An action or event making a significant change or stage of development"

Journey (n.) 1200 "A defined course of traveling; one's path in life"

Race - 1774, With much definition on this, lets just say in this case it represent "tribe, nation or clan of various people" Collective thoughts of the human race.

An age had passed; the gate unto another age flies open at the touch of time –

The gate was open for the Piscean Age for the entrance of the Avatar Yeshua (Jesus). The Pisces is the last zodiac sign and the symbol of two fish swimming in opposite directions. This represents the dualism of man's finite consciousness and the infinite consciousness of universe, material man versus spiritual man, and the conflict between the ego-self. Pisces is located in the 12th and final house of the chart, a place of secrets and invisibility, and Neptune is the ruling plane. Yeshua was here completing the age of Spiritual redemption.

Immanuel (Heb.) - Immanu –El "Jehovah is with us" It is also a title.

Gospel (n.) - "Good message"

Carnal (adj.) c. 1400 "Physical, human, mortal"

Revealers (v.) late 14c."Make (previously unknown or secret information) known to others."

Light (n.) mid- 15c. - The understanding principal in mind. In divine order it always comes first into consciousness. Light is a symbol of wisdom.

The inner illumination of spirit in the center of every human being. The Light is The Divine Truth."

Soul on Fire - When the soul is allowed its full expression, the soul encourages one to seek their spiritual pursuits. Once the fire has evolved within the mind it can never be extinguished.

Holy Zeal – "Great energy in pursuit of a cause or an objective" also "A noble passion. Intensity; the inward fire of the soul that urges one to go onward.

Conscious – "This is first heaven" and heaven is a state of mind. The conscious mind is masculine (Body-Belief) your conscious mind is what you think. This is your rational, logical mind it is masculine in nature and operates personally, selectively and judgmentally. Your conscious mind creates and develops your thoughts. Your thoughts have two aspects: the idea – the statement of the thought, and the feelings associated with the thought. Your conscious mind transmit your thoughts to your <u>subconscious</u> mind though the feeling aspect of the thought. It proceeds to conclusions based on observation, experience, and education. (The conscious mind represents the world of effect).

Mission (n.) 1590 "An important assignment carried out" To go out in the world and teach the Truth.

Tore (Tear) (v.) late 13c. "Sense of "to pull by force" (away from some situation or attachment)

Debase (v.) 1560's "The lower value of self" to reduce (something) in quality or value; degrade.

Restore (v.) c. 1300 "To give back," also "to build up again, repair,"

Naught (n.) - "Nothing"

He has clothed His son in Flesh – Elihu spoke these words indicating to Mary that her son was clothed in flesh is in reference to characteristics of the Universal Creator in which he has the opportunity to learn and excel from the Divine Education from the sacred schools. Clothed in flesh also represent the garment of Salvation. The meaning in connection with the statement "Son of God" means the fullness of the perfect-man idea in Divine Mind, the Higher Self. <u>The true spiritual self of every individual.</u>

Son signifies creation from two principles of masculine and feminine from an infinite point of view. It also denotes a manifestation of the first cause of all from which Allah has created. We are all sons and daughters (Creation).

Savior (n.) c. 1300 "One who delivers or rescues from peril"

Love – c. 1500 "The highest energy" cannot be defined from a finite point of view. Those who embrace it can only feel it.

Prepared (v.) mid-15c."Make ready beforehand"

Rend (v.) - "To tear, cut down"

Lofty (adj.) early 15c."Exalted, of high rank" also "with a high purpose"

Hill – 1570s a hill symbolize to climb to a higher attainment, wider view of life or opportunity.

Valleys – c. 1300 Valley is home and sanctuaries, the place where we make our living and fulfill our dreams. It is the symbol of new life. Valleys provide a safe place to test our -selves and develop our skills. Time spent in a valley can trigger opportunities to help others or to become something greater than our goals and ambitions.

Purity (n.) c. 1200 "Simple truth" also "clean, pure, unmixed; uncorrupted, clear"

Purity is the result of continued spiritual harmony with Allah, recognize the necessity of maintain our spiritual vision through personal purity. Purity is the process through which the life-rhythm manifests; the rhythm of that indwelling spirit. For its effort, though all these experiences, is to arrive at that realization where it finds itself pure, pure in essence and pure from all that could affect its original condition.

Comprehend (v.) mid-14c. "To perceive mentally"

Remembrance (n.) late 14c. As "Consideration, reflection; present consciousness of a past event; store of personal experiences available to recollection, capacity to recall the past."

Registry (n.) late 15c."Act of registering;" meaning "book of record"

Open Book – Signifies: "If book is open you will learn something new" "when a book is closed you need to research something" A book is the material incarnation of knowledge and wisdom. It contains the central doctrine of nearly every existing religion. Also an open book depicts the book of life.

Deed (n.) - "A doing, act, action, transaction, event"

Messenger – c. 1200 Spiritual thoughts that always bring messages of light.

Language (n.) late 13c."Pronunciations and arrangement of sounds used to express thoughts"

Native land – Meaning the land of the original people. That in which is "natural, hereditary, connected with something in a natural way" Therefore we are the living deed on every soil where we set foot on.

CHAPTER III

ELIHU'S LESSON-THE UNITY OF LIFE

THE Unity of Life is which is shown in man's social, moral and mental attitude. The national and religious codes are often very strict with regard to this kind of life, and sometimes it is merely an external, which the individual soul has to break through to find that of a higher self. Unity implies state of oneness.

Pupil (n.) late 14c."Student" Training in ethical self-discipline, which means learning to restrain from acting, speaking, or thinking destructively.

Every living thing is bound by cords to every other living thing - Cords are made of astral and etheric energy and is basically a connection between the astral and etheric bodies of two or more beings, which allows for an exchange of emotional and / or etheric energy. This is much like an umbilical cord that transfers emotional energy and it does not matter how far away the other person is, as the cord is not a physical substance and distance is irrelevant, so it is still effective from the other side of the planet.

They will not do to other men what they would not have other men do unto them –

Ancient Egypt – "That which you hate to be done to you, do not do to another."

Ancient China – "Never impose on others what you would not choose for yourself." Confucius (c. 500 BC)

Ancient India – "Treat others as you treat yourself."

Ancient Persia – "That nature alone is good which refrains from doing another whatsoever is not good for itself."

Unto (prep.) mid-13c."Until"

The Higher Self and Lower self – The Higher Self is the Higher Mind and the lower self is the lower mind. The lower self creates illusion, which is separation from Allah

(The only Truth) It will have you believing the most unreasonable things. It will make you believe you are not the guilty one when you are, and it will reason with you to try and get you to see its point of view.

It will even argue with your Higher Self, and if you are not at a <u>Higher rate of vibration</u>, you're Higher Self will not be able to retaliate with the lower self. When one has then raised one's vibration to a higher level (Higher Self) It is then one can see through the illusion of the lower self, and even see the reason as the why things are happening to them. When one has no emotional response to what is happening around, then one will feel free the bondage of the lower self.

Refection (n.) late 14c."Serious thought or consideration, contemplation, thinking, deliberation, and thought"

Distorted (v.) 1580s "Giving a misleading or false account or impression; misrepresented"

Murky ethers of the flesh "Not transmitting or reflecting light or radiant energy"

Illusion (n.) mid-14c."Act of deception" also "a thing that is likely to be wrongly perceived or interpreted by the senses"

Embodiment (n.) 1824."A representation or expression of something definite or visible form"

Reverse (adj.) c. 1300. "Opposite"

Justice (n.) mis-12c."Quality of being fair and just" also "righteous person or persons" is from late 14c.

Mercy (n.) 13c."Disposition to forgive or show compassion"

Right (adj.) - "Morally correct," and "just, righteous, wise"

Breed (v.) c. 1200 "Bring to birth" or produces, development, growth.

Hatred (n.) early 13c."Intense, dislike, or ill will" characterized by Lucifer this is mental. Characterized by Lucifer this is mental

Slander (n.) late 13c. "The action or crime of making a false spoken statement damaging to a persons character" Characterized by the Dragon this is socially.

Lewdness (adj.) early 13c."Ignorant, uneducated, unlearned" also early 13c, descended to "coarse, vile, lustful" Characterized by Satan this is moral.

Murder (n.) c. 1300 "Unlawful killing" also "mortal sin, crime; punishment, torment, misery" Characterized by the beast this physical

Theft (n.) mid-13c."The action or crime of stealing" Characterized by the Devil this economic.

Mother of the Virtues – "Act of the Divine Feminine Energy force in all natural bodies in keeping the behavior in high moral standards with all its divine qualities"

Harmonies of life – "Bringing balance in ones life" Harmony from which comes individual power, which manifest throughout the universe and is reflected within us.

Poorly (adj.) early 13c."Inadequately, badly, insufficiently" meaning "in ill health is from 1750.

Gain (n.) late 15c."That which has been acquired" (possession, resources, wealth)

Unrest (n.) mid-14c."State of dissatisfaction, disturbance in a person"

Misery (n.) late 14c."A state of feeling external unhappiness," also "mental distress or discomfort of the mind." From 1530s, "Body pain" is 1825.

Death (n.) - "The death of the light and life of spirit in man's consciousness. Death is the absence of life in the body."

Apple (n.) - "Apple symbolized as an erotic form" A fruit that signifies carnal pleasure.

Pleasant (adj.) late 14c."Pleasing, agreeable"

Core (n.) late 14c."Heart"

Bitterness (adj.) - "Anger, hostility, spite, grudge, friction, venom, hatred, malice"

Gall (n.) - "Disrespect, boldness" or "Embittered spirit"

Study (n.) c. 1300 "Application of the mind to the acquisition of knowledge" also "A detailed investigation and examination of a subject or situation." A state of deep thought or contemplation.

Ransomed (v.) early 14c. "A deliverance or rescue from punishment from sin"

Perils – "Serious and immediate danger"

Seek (v.) - "Inquire, search for; pursue; long for, wish for, desire; look for"

Salvation (n.) c.1200 "The returning of man to his spiritual birthright; regaining conscious possession of his Universal Creator given attributes. It comes as the result of redemption; the change from (sin) wrongful thinking to thinking on a righteous level. And from this one is on the path to Freedom."

Evil (adj.) - "Unreality; error thought; a product of the fallen human consciousness"

Deem (v.) - "Think or believes to be"

Monster (n.) early 14c. "A repulsive character, awful deed" also "person of inhuman cruelty" It symbolize the latent and dangerous forces, in a greater or lesser state if freedom, of the human unconscious in its aggressive and dreadful aspect.

Netherworld (n.) 1630s "The part of society engaged in crime and vice"

Gods that are but demons – Godlike person of a demon, which represents error states of mind the have negative thoughts.

Disguise (n.) c. 1400 "One to deceive"

Powerful (adj.) c. 1400 "Of great quality or number"

Yet (adj.) c. 1200 "Till now, thus far, earlier, at last, also"

Full (adj.) early 14c. "Containing all that can be received"

Jealousy (n.) c. 1200 "The state of feeling envy, resentment, bitterness, suspicion, distrust"

Lust (v.) c. 1200 "To wish, to desire in a negative way"

Whose (pron.) - "Who"

Favors (v.) mid-14c. "To regard with favor, indulge, treat with preconception"

Bought (v.) - "Acquire or exchange for something"

Costly (adj.) –late 13c."Causing suffering, lost, or disadvantage"

Sacrifice (n.) late 13c."Offering of something (especially a life)."

No ears to hear – One that will not listen to the Truth.

No eyes to see – Eyes are probably the most important symbolic sensory organs. They can represent clairvoyance, omniscience, and/or a gateway into the soul. Other qualities the eyes associated with are: intelligence, light, vigilance, moral conscience, and truth.

No Heart to Sympathize – A thoughtless thinker with no compassion.

No power to save – One that has no positive energy to keep safe or rescue (someone or something) from harm or danger.

Myth (n.) 1830 "A widely held but false belief or idea" also "anything delivered byword of mouth, of unknown origin. Other meanings of words for myth are Folk tale, tale, story, lore, and folklore.

Clothed with the shadow of a thought – Shadows are often identified with a person's soul, and they are considered "dark entities with a nature all of their own" Shadows are the unconscious layers of personality that are integrated into the structure of the "experienced world" only through the process of individuation.

Dethroned (v.) c. 1600 "Remove from power"

Exalted (v.) late 14c."Of a person or status placed at a high or powerful level"

Throne of power – In the Egyptian system of hieroglyph; the throne is a developmental sign embracing the concepts of supports, exaltation, equilibrium and security. By containing this level of power one will have control over their thoughts and feelings. The mind and body have power to transform energy from one plane of consciousness to another. In mind, power is increased through exalted ideas. When one co-operates with their Principles he/she will sit on the throne of their authority and the elemental force is subject to you.

David and Goliath – The invisible battle within, as David meaning "Beloved one," and Goliath meaning "Rebellion" The battle between David and Goliath can be seen as the battle between physical or worldly power and spiritual power; between sense driven consciousness and that consciousness aligned with the Divine. David represents the energy of dominion applied to guide thoughts, emotions and actions with divine ideas rather than the fearful ideas of our material world.

Goliath represents a power struggle while David represents an opportunity for overcoming a challenge. Goliath the giant represents a major obstacle keeping the spiritual self from growth. David, the spiritual side, must overcome this obstacle in order to control the sinful sensory thoughts. They also represent the battle of the dark, negative thoughts and emotions versus the thoughts and emotions that are light, as light/dark, conscious/unconscious, and awareness/denial/ wake/sleep. One must fight these negative thoughts and emotions if not thereby one may become more a more consumed by them.

Mind often thinks it is in control, when actually, it is all just a grand illusion, created by the same mind that creates this black and white duality and all of the inner and outer friction/strife that results from this. The David must learn to let go and surrender, totally and completely, therefore eliminating all frictions. Spiritual has to overcome the material, or that "Truth must over come errors in living.

We do not slay the ego by our own might or strength. That would mean the ego is driving again and it would never work. We need to simply realize to become conscious of what the ego is through activities like meditation. Then the spirit within us will naturally take over. When Goliath of the dark has been slain, you become conscious of a greater reality and this will be your savior, love upon your throne.

End Notes

This was a Three-year course of study under the teachings of Elihu and Salome.

CHAPTER IV

DEATH AND BURIAL OF ELIZABETH-MATHENO'S LESSONS-THE MINISTRY OF DEATH

MINISTRY, which means Holy Instructions, therefore one has to be instructed from a pure thought about the physical death of the body and not the Spirit within the form.

Matheno – "Gift of Thoth" Matheno was the High Priest of the temple of Sakara.

John was twelve years old – which means he was about to go through his rite of passage. Within the ceremonies he will mark an important transitional period of his life, such as entering manhood, marriage, having children and death. These rites involve ritual activities and teachings designed to strip individuals of their original roles and prepare them for new roles.

Grieved (v.) c. 1200 "Cause a great deal of sorrow" also "sadden, stress, mourn"

Binds (v.) - "Cohere or cause to cohere in a single mass"

Boat – The boat represents a journey, a crossing, adventure, and exploration. It is also the femininity and "sheltering aspect of the Great Mother"

Worth (adj.) c. 1200 "Significant, valuable, of value; appreciated, highly thought-of, deserving, honorable, noble"

Task (n.) early 14c. "A quantity of labor imposed as a duty"

Solve (v.) late 14c. "Find an answer to, explanation for, or means of effectively dealing with (a problem or mystery)."

Selfishness (adj.) 1630 "A person lacking consideration for others; concerned chiefly with one's own personal self"

Noble (adj.) c. 1200 "Illustrious, distinguished; worthy of honor or respect"

Inspiration (n.) c. 1300 "A inflow of Divine ideas" also "activity of a spiritual character"

Crisis (n.) early 15c. "A time of intense difficulty" also "A critical point, turning point or a important change takes place"

Conception (n.) early 14c. "The way in which something is perceived or regarded" Mental sense "process of forming concepts. Also "That which is conceived in the mind" from 1520's.

Sages (n.) mid-14c. "Man of profound wisdom" Originally applied to the 7 sages.

Elijah (Heb.) - "My G-d is YAHWEH" Elijah a Hebrew prophet of the 9th century BC, Elijah (the spiritual I AM) represents the guardian and administrator of the Divine Law.

Messiah (n.) c. 1300 "A liberator, leader or savior of a particular group or cause"

Harbinger (n.) late 15c. "A person or thing that announces or signal the approach of another" also "A forerunner of something"

Pave (v.) early 14c. "To prepare or make easier" also "To pave the way for future development"

Readiness (n.) mid-14 "The state of being fully prepared for something"

Word (n.) c. 1200 "A single distinct meaningful element of speech or writing"

Deeds (n.) - "An action that is performed intentionally or consciously"

Infancy (n.) late 14c. "Condition of babyhood," also "childhood" And could mean any age up to 21.

Vow (n.) c. 1300 "Solemn promise" a promise to G-d, dedication; that which is promised; a wish, desire, longing, prayer. Devote oneself to a religious order or life.

Nazarite - (Nazarene) c 1200 "Holy man" The Nazarenes were a sect of the Essenes.

Wine nor fiery drinks — Wine symbolized to be the fluid of the blood of death, and is typically associated with its powers of intoxication. Wine is also alcohol, which is called a fiery drink. Because it signifies fire and water the conjunction of opposites.

A state of creation and destruction.

Pattern (n.) early 14c."Outline, plan, model" also "model of behavior"

Path (n.) - "Course of action" or "direction"

Point (v.) late 14c. "The point signifies unity, the Origin and the Centre" It also represents the principles of manifestation and sending something out.

Teacher (n.) c. 1300 "A teacher or mentor instructs, guides, or helps another in process of gaining understanding, knowledge, or skills"

Treads (n.) early 13c."A step or walk a specified way"

Footprints (n.) 1550s, "Footprints symbolize the way of Divine Prophets, Sages, and Master teachers" The footprint is a very ancient and sacred symbol. It represents memory, and the teachings, of the Master Teacher. The footprint reminds us that these Master Teachers once resided in our earthly domain and shared Divine Wisdom with us. Let this be known that footprints implies (In the law of evidence).

And although these Master teachers are gone their Teachings, Their Footprints remains with us. And although these Teachings may be called by many different names, the essence of these teachings is the same everywhere.

These Teachings, These Footprints, are available to each and every one of us. These Teachings are the Divine, Universal Wisdom handed down to each and every one of us, freely, by the Ancient Masters for us to study, absorb and use in a way that is most compatible with our very own Divine Nature.

Master (n.) 1740s "Chief, head, director, teacher" An Enlightened Master possesses inherent knowledge (rather than learned knowledge); that is, He or she literally knows everything of the natural world and how inventions arise from that. He or she knows how the universe is formed- past, present and future, and how the karma of all life forms are intertwined within it.

A Master in this present life is one who attained enlightenment in a previous life, which is why the knowledge they possess now is inherent (realized), rather than newly required. An enlighten Master always works to empower their students and to serves others by aiming to the deeper truth of essential Being.

Inner Life – Inner life represents, today, modern culture, which has been exaggerated outward appearance by all the means of mass media. People lives have been laid bare for all to see. And what we see we do unknowingly.

Ceremonies (n.) late 14c."The ritual observances and procedures performed at grand and formal occasions, a formal religious or public occasion, typically celebrating a particular event or anniversary"

Sins - "Wrongful thinking" and moral wrongdoings.

Rite (n.) early 14c. The rites and ceremonies of priests in the temple represent the action of spiritual forces in developing the body

Water - Water represent material cleansing and Fire represents spiritual cleansing. Water cleansing is a symbolic way to wash away external character.

This rite of cleansing is a preparation rite - This is our Purification Rites. Act 7- All Moorish Americans must keep their hearts and minds pure with love, and their bodies clean with water.

Israel – Meaning "El Persevereth"

Reform (v.) c. 1300 Meaning, "to bring (a person) away from evil course of life"

Temple - "Body"

Multitudes (n.) early 14c. "A great number, a crowd, the common people" also "many, much"

Tis - mid-15c. Contraction of it is.

Jericho (Heb.) - "Place of fragrance" Jericho express relative terms; that is, they stand in a state of dependence on the Absolute. The word expresses the elemental soul, life, mind, spirit—reflected breath and mind, the outer, intellectual –in contrast to the inner spirit. Jericho signifies the intellect, an external or reflected state of consciousness

Tarried (v.) early 14c. "Stay longer than intended; delay leaving a place"

Jordan (Heb.) - "The descended; the descending one" Jordan represents the life current. Wash in the Jordan (life stream) because, as man's spiritual perception reveals to him the realities of life, he is convinced of the need of cleansing the personal will. Spiritual I AM commands the denial of material beliefs and limitations. When the will is under the direction of Spirit the mind and body express their natural purity and perfection.

Wilderness c. 1200, (n.) The word signifies what is little inhabited and cultivated, and also signifies what is not at all inhabited and cultivated.

Engedi (Heb.) - "Eye or fountain of happiness" Engedi was a town, also called the city of palm trees. At a later period Engedi was the gathering place of the Moabites and Ammonites.

Temple of Sakara – Sakara is Indian-Todas language. Sakara is a derivative of the mane Sakari which mean "Sweet one" Sakara is best know for the step pyramid, the oldest know of Egypt's 97 pyramids. The architect and genius Imhoptep built it for King Djoser of the 3rd Dynasty.

Valley of the Nile – The largest river in the world. The Nile is the "international" river as eleven countries share its water resources. Its primary source is Egypt and Sudan. The Nile has two major branches, the White Nile and the Blue Nile.

Hicrophant (n.) 1670s "Expounder of sacred mysteries" or "one who shows sacred things, to reveal, brings to light, "expounder of esoteric doctrines" from 1822. Also Esoteric teacher at the Ancient Mysteries.

Eighteen – 18/9 the 1 refers to the self, its accomplishments. The 8 refer to physical endurance, rhythm and movement.

Wrought (adj.) - "Worked"

Temple Gates – The gate is an entryway into an unknown place, or a place of great significance; it is a threshold, and may connect the living and the dead. (Thoughts) In many cultures, passing through a gateway signifies a right of passage.

Master Mind – "A mind that has been free and open to Divine instinct of ideas and guidance"

End Notes

Initiation ritual involving the use of water.

In Buddhism, purity directly effects man's ability to "see" truth, and "listen" to the voice of truth. Man needs that purity in order to be attached to Truth, and realize gradual spiritual growth.

The significance of water in Zoroastrianism is a combination of its purifying properties and its importance as a fundamental life element.

Water in Hinduism is sacred it has a special place because it is believed to have spiritually cleansing powers. This relates to both physical cleanliness and spiritual well being.

In Judaism ritual washing is intended to restore or maintain a state of ritual purity.

In Islam, the purification of the senses also corresponds to purification of spiritual entity. As such it is an integral part of the spiritual growth. The discipline of purification practices is so rich with symbols where each sense refers to a spiritual dimension.

It is well to note that the primary textbooks of Alexandrine School were Matheno's books. Because the very first professors of the Alexandrine School were the Egyptian Priests.

Chapter V

After the Feast-The Homeward Journey-The missing Jesus-The Search for Him-His Parents Find Him in the Temple-He Goes With Them to Nazareth-Symbolic Meaning of Carpenter's Tools

Esoteric lessons of tools.

THE great Feast of the Pasch – On this day the fourteenth, the first-born son of each family, if he were above thirteen, fast in memory of the deliverance of the first-born of the Israelites. The Nazarenes the sect of the Essenes were observing this day.

Journey (v.) mid-14c. "Travel from one place to another" Symbolically, it is a spiritual adventure, designed to explore the Self until serenity is achieved. Desire for discovery or change is inherent.

Samaria (Heb.) - "Watcher; guard" Intellectual perception, the department of the objective consciousness that functions through the head (watcher) Samaria is a city in Palestine, built on a mountain. It was the capitol of the kingdom of Israel.

Sought – Past tense and participle of seek. Seek (v.) "Search for"

Kindred (n.) c. 1200 "Family, linage; nation, tribe, people, blood relations"

Galilee (Heb.) - "Turning, a ring, a circle, a circuit, rolling energy i. e., momentum."

Galilee signifies as the Energy of life, life activity; soul energy; power, force, energy, acting in conjunction with substance. The location of Galilee was in a region of northern Israel. The northern most part of Palestine and the ancient kingdom of Israel.

Zebedee (Heb.) - "Jehovah has given; Jah is endower" Zebedee was the husband of Salome (not Salome the teacher) but the sister of Mary.

Disputing (v.) c. 1300 "Discuss, explain"

Doctor of the law - Doctor (n.) c. 1300 "A teacher of the law" law (n.) "Ordinance, rule prescribed by authority, regulation; district governed by the same laws" also something laid down, that which is fixed or set.

Pressed the Hand – Meaning transforming with the intent of trust and peace within you. Note: this not shaking hand.

Carpenter – A Spiritual mentor who helps us meticulously build, reconstruct and alter the Thoughts, Lessons and philosophies that are the building materials of our Inner Temple.

Tools – This signifies the Spiritual tools, which are non-material and are used to affect change within self. The approach has is that each tool has three parts:

1. Description: An overview of the tool and when it is best used
2. Principle: A list of principles behind the tools
3. Action: Suggest a practical program of action to affect attitude or awareness toward greater Quality of Life.

Work Shop of the Mind – The workshop of the mind signifies to investigate his/her thinking, learning and understanding ones character through metaphysics.

Numerology and Symbolic Meaning of The Tools of The Mind

Square 27/9 - Spiritual insight. Compassionate. Brotherly love. 2 add a loving & cooperative quality. 7 adds poise & reserve and desire for study & perfection. 9 represent humanity. Symbolic: The Square, as the expression of the four parts of mans psychotically, its form gives the impression of firmness and stability, and this explains its frequent use in symbols of organization and construction.

Compass 23/5 – Adaptable. Clever. Alert desire for freedom to explore & enjoy life. Five represent the five senses. Symbolic: An emblematic representation of the act of creation, found in allegories of geometry, architecture and equity. It also symbolizes the power of measurement, of delimitation. (Choices made by the researcher, that you which describe the boundaries, that you have set to study). This is the place to explain: the things that you are not doing (and why you have chosen not to do them). Compass points in symbology are, East-within (spiritual) West-without (expression) North-above (intellect) South-below (physical)

Axe 25/7 – Wise, Silent, Scientific. Thinks deeply about things & will analyzes and decide for yourself. Symbolic: A symbol of the power of light. It is a symbol of spiritual penetration and fertilization, as it opens the ground. Also it is a symbol of celestial illumination.

Hammer 31/4 – Accurate. Conscientious. Organized. Patient. Prudent. Practical. Sincere. Studious. Loyal. Symbolic: Hammer is essentially a masculine force, and when striking or crushing it represents justice. The hammer is not only a tool; it represents might. They use it for destruction, protection and fertilization, but it also symbolizes immortality.

Plane 21/3 – Enthusiastic. Expressive. Optimistic. Symbolic: Plane has a special status of a clear thinking level as in the term (level headed person). Which means one who can think positive. The symbol of one who "to smooth, level off; wipe away, erase" their negative thoughts.

Chisel 29/11 –The 29 behind the 11 stands for spiritual power. They represent the positive –negative, masculine-feminine, active-passive forces-that by walking between the two of them we bring a sense of balance into our lives. 11 is The Psychic Master. Creative. Dignified. High idea. Inspired. Quiet. Reserved. Teacher. Wants to uplift people (as a whole, not necessarily individually). The 2 is peace, cooperation, loving service. The 9 is humanity, universal, universal service, and brt0herly love. Symbolic: To cut and shape one character out of lower mental thoughts into higher productive humble manner.

Line 22 - The 22 knows how to unite the inspirational idea with the physical manifestation. 22 are The Master Architect. A master of accomplishment. A very capable leader. Dynamic. Organized. Practical. Symbolic: The line divide, measures, and binds; a straight line is infinite, and may symbolize the path to man's destiny. When the line is horizontal, it reflects the temporal world, and when vertical it reflects the spiritual real.

Plummet 28/1 – One is the line between Heaven and Earth, the creative power, the First cause touching the Earth plane. Active. Good mind. Determination. Willpower. 1 I am Exclusive. Symbolic: The plumb rule is an instrument of antiquity. One is to avoid dissimulation in conversation and, to direct your steps in the path, which leads to immortality. This idea of the immortal life was always connected in symbology with that of the perpendicular-something that rose directly upward.

Saw 7 – Deep thinker. Intuitive. Knowledgeable. Logical. Spiritual. Conduct of "Saying, discourse, speech, study, tradition, and tale"

Ladder – The ladder represents the step-by step realization by means of which man assimilates the divine ideas of Truth that come to him from Allah.

Twelve Step Ladder – Holy Instruction for Thy Children Chapter 23

1. Obedience – Conforming to the 7 universal laws and the 5 principles.
2. Modesty – Humbleness (Accessing higher dimensions of life)
3. Gratitude – Appreciations (Perceiving life beyond logic)
4. Charity - Love
5. Temperance – Self restraint (Remove negative)
6. Prudence – Common sense (Clarity of perception)
7. Justice – Non-judgmental (Activity of appealing directly to the divine law)
8. Sincerity – Truthful (Developing an inclusive consciousness)
9. Diligence – Resolution
10. Benevolence - Compassion
11. Science – Systematic knowledge of laws and principles.
12. Religion – Return to the original knowledge of self.

End Notes

Trinity of steps is 3 and the 4 opening of the brakes of circle equals 12. (3X4)=12

All Feast represent spiritual teachings.

CHAPTER VI

LIFE AND WORKS OF JESUS IN INDIA AMONG THE MOSLEMS

RAVANNA - "Raven" signifies the vision and foresight to be able to organize others and to hold positions of responsibility with poise and self-confidence.

Feasts (n.) c. 1200 all the feast and festivities of the Jews had their foundation in divine science, although the people may not have understood their significance. These feast were related to the spiritual life of the people.

Brahmin Priest – Brahmin priest are the highest of the four Hindu castes. They were known as the spiritual and intellectual leaders of the society.

Jewish Priest – The Priest at the Temple of Jerusalem not only officiated over religious life of the people, they were also rulers, and judges.

Chief Hill El - Chief (n.) c 1300 "Head leader, captain, ruler," of something. Hillel (Heb.) meaning "Praise" Hill El was a Chief of the Jewish Priest of the Holy Temple of Jerusalem. Yeshua (Jesus) was a student of Hill El for one year.

Whence (adv. conj.) early 13c."From what place or source" also "From which, from where"

Day Star – "Which precedes and accompanies the sun-rising" This is the planet of Love which is Venus. Venus can appear up to 47 degrees away fro the Sun. During these times, when it rises or sets a few hours before or after the Sun, it can be seen just before sunrise or just after sunset as a bright Morning or Evening Star. The reason Venus always precedes or follows the Sun in the sky, is that she is interior (sometimes called inferior) planet, that is, she is closer to the Sun than the earth is. Because Venus rotates one hundred and eighty degrees on its polar axis between inferior conjunctions. The extraordinary feature of Venus cycle, is it has a remarkable pattern forcefully emerges a Five-Pointed Star!

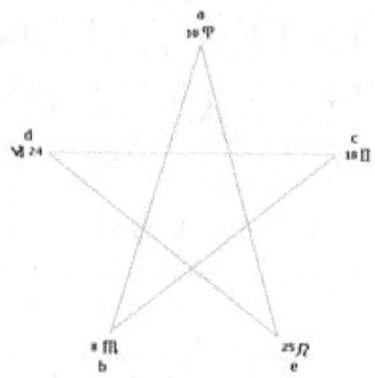

The diagram above plots five consecutive inferior conjunctions of Venus.

This five-pointed Start also represents the Star in our Moorish Flag.

Day Star signifies to bring in an absolute sense, a way or gate said to lead somewhere into moral and spiritual light and knowledge, which enlighten the mind.

Magian Priest – Magian Priest were of ancient Persia of the Median tribe. They were Zoroastrians and the Priest of the Prophet Zarathustra.

Flight (n.) c. 1200 "Act of fleeing"

Prophesies c. 1200 "Function of a prophet"

Wonders (n.) late 13c. "Marvelous thing, miracle, object of astonishment"

Wrath (n.) - "Anger"

Serving with His Father as a carpenter - Serving as a Spiritual mentor with his father Joseph.

Entranced (v.) 1590s. "Someone with amazement and delight, holding their entire attention"

Train (n.) early 14c. "A succession of pack animals traveling in the same direction" Also as a caravan, convoy and trail.

Engaged (adj.) 1610s "Occupied"

Dwellings (n.) mid-14c. "A place of residence"

Sons of Men - "Sons of Humanity"

Hands – Hands can increase the flow of universal life energy into our bodies. The hands are the power of magnetism. Also represents executive ability; the doing of things; outer or manual power.

Compass, Square, and Ax – Compass (Spiritual Movement) – Square (Honesty) – Ax (Strength)

Marmion Way was a small place in Nazareth, the capital and largest city in the Northern district of Israel.

Great (adj.) - "Of an extent, amount, or intensity considerably above the normal or average"

Patron (n.) c. 1300 "A protector" Also "a person who gives support to a person"

Consent (n.) c. 1300 "Approval"

Rising Sun - Sun rising from the East meaning within the Spiritual. The dawn of the new day or new age.

Crossed the Sand - Symbolize your journey through life

Provinces (n.) early 14c. "An area of special knowledge, interest" also "Territory, region, country"

Orissa – A state in India, located on the east coast of India, by the Bay of Bengal. Also known as Odisha.

Temple of Jagannath – A sacred Hindu Temple dedicated to Jagannath and located on the eastern coast of India at Puri in the state of Orissa. The temple of Jagannath in Puri is regarded as one of the Char Dham (sacred Hindu pilgrimage places) in India. Yeshua (Jesus) was accepted as a pupil and he study there for four years.

Vedas – Vedas meaning knowledge is an ancient sacred Hindu scripture written in early Sanskrit 1200 BCE to 100 CE. The four chief collections are the Rig Veda, Sama Veda, Yajur Veda, and Atharva Veda

Manic law – Manic means unbalance and the meaning of unbalance in

Hindi is a lack of balance or state of instability. Manic law is the awareness of an unbalance mindset (beliefs that affect somebody's attitude).

Conception (n.) early 14c. "Act of conceiving in the mind, grasp, comprehension"

Amaze (v.) early 13c. "Sense of overwhelm with wonder, Impress, and astonish"

End Notes

Honorable mention 'Upanishad' from the Vedas (Books of Knowledge) the word Upanishad means, "to sit down near," bringing to mind pupils gathering around their teacher for philosophical instruction.

CHAPTER VII

THE FRIENDSHIP OF JESUS AND LAMAAS-JESUS EXPLAINS TO LAMAAS THE MEANING OF TRUTH

THE path of Friendship teaches us sincerity, gratitude, sympathy, sensitivity, and appreciation. A person begins his spiritual accomplishment by learning how to be a friend. The first lesson on the spiritual path that one has to learn is the manner of friendship. Once that is learned then all other parts of spiritual journey will become easy. The relationship with members of your family, teacher, student, all these need a spirit behind them a connection and that connection is the spirit of Friendship.

Plaza (n.) c. 1200 "Place, spot, open space, courtyard"

Lamas - "A priest or monk a title of respect applied to a spiritual leader in Tibetan Buddhism. Lamas attributes are having an executive abilities and leadership. He is moral, balanced, honest, intellectual, bold, independent, spiritual, inquisitive and

interested in research. Wise and practical, always think before he act.

Brahmas – In Hindi the meaning: Born to the highest caste. Indian meaning "Absolute"

In all the world there are two things the one is Truth, the other is falsehood –

This is also one of the 7 Universal Laws "Polarity" Everything is dual; everything has poles; everything has its pair of opposites. There are two sides to everything, and every truth may also be false. We experience this duality throughout life.

Truth – The Absolute; that which accords with Allah as a divine principle; that which is has been, and ever will be; that which is eternally is. The Truth of Allah is reality.

The great truth is that man is a spiritual being, who brings with him a life to unfold, a power to release, a love to express. He doesn't begin life empty, but as a dynamic spiritual potentiality.

Falsehood – "Deceptive thoughts that have been built up by error, selfish desires"

Falsehood that which seems to be – Something that was never true, but it was believed to be true and because it was believed to be true, you believed it into your existence and this became your truth. It is really false (lie) posing as truth.

Seems (v.) c. 1200 "To appear to be" Give the impression or sensation of being something or having a particular quality.

Ought (n.) "All " the symbol for ought is 0 there is no beginning and there is no ending.

Naught (n.) c. 1400 "nothing"

Reflexes (n.) c. 1500 "Reflection of light"

Strangely (adj.) late 13c. "From elsewhere, unknown, unfamiliar" or "as a result of being out of one's natural environment"

Mix (v.) 1530s "Composed of more than one element, of mixed nature"

Vibrate (v.) 1610 One of the Seven Universal Laws "Vibration" Nothing is stationary; everything vibrates. "Move to and fro" set in tremulous motion, move quickly to and fro.

Conditions (v.) late 15c. "The state of something, especially with regard to its appearance, quality, or working order."

Conjoined (v.) late 14c. "Meet, come together"

Strive (v.) c. 1200 "Make great efforts to achieve or something"

Abides (v.) "Remain"

Power (n.) c. 1300 "Ability, ability to act or do, strength, vigor, might"

Manifest (adj.) late 14c."Clearly revealed" Also evident, obvious and noticeable.

Result (n.) 1640s "Outcome, effect"

Force (n.) c. 1300 "Universal life force" Spiritual energy.

Omnipotent (adj.) early 14."Almighty, all-powerful"

Directed (v.) c. 1500 "To govern, regulate"

Power in the winds – Wind is East life currents that come from within and surround the whole being; the executive power of mind clearing the way to higher states of consciousness.

Power in the waves – An inner work as in a fine tune to the heart (soul) and senses to perceive the spiritual world. Like a radio receiver detecting airwaves as the buttons are turned. Thus one tunes oneself becoming more and more attuned to the spiritual frequency through actions called "intent" Until a new dimension suddenly opens and the spiritual world appears.

Power in the lightning stroke – Represents "force, light, and power"

Power in the human Arm - Represents the capacity and ability to hold the experiences of life.

Power in the eye – Spiritual vision; intuitive seeing with the eye of Truth.

Ether/Ethereal (adj.) 1510s."Of the highest regions of the atmosphere" One of the celestial spheres.

Elohim (Heb.) c. 1600, "Creative Spirits"

Angel (n.) 14c."A spiritual being believed to act as an attendant, agent, or messenger of Allah, represented in human form. Mal'akh Hebrew "messenger (of Jehovah)

Man (n.) - Human being, person (male or female) in general.

The Rock – Signifies the faith within you. The rock is not material it is mental. A mind receptive to spiritual truth and spiritual substance.

Gnosis ((n.) 1703, "Knowledge", especially "special knowledge of spiritual mysteries" or Higher knowledge of spiritual things.

Knowledge (n.) late 14c."Capacity for knowing, understanding; experience" also "fact or condition of knowing, awareness of a fact;" also news, notice, information, and learning.

Sensing (v) 1590s "To perceive by the senses," also to be conscious inwardly of (ones state or condition) 1from 1680s.

Wisdom (n.) Intuitive knowing; spiritual intuition; the voice within as the source of our understanding; mental action based on the Divine Truth within. Wisdom includes judgment, discrimination, intuition, and all the departments of mind that come under the head of knowing. Knowing is the capacity that transcends intellectual knowledge. Spiritual judgment always places wisdom above the other faculties of the mind and reveals that knowledge and intelligence are auxiliary to understanding.

Consciousness - "This is second heaven" and heaven is a state of mind. Wisdom (She/Holy Breath) The subconscious mind - Feminine – Heart (Soul-Faith) Your subconscious mind represents what you are. It is your emotional, feeling mind. It is Feminine in nature and operates impersonally, non-selectively, and non-judgmentally. (The subconscious mind represents The world of cause) your subconscious mind accepts every idea as true, and gives it form and expression through feeling.

That heaven and earth and hell are not above, around below, but in; - 7 Universal Law of the principle of Correspondence "As above so below; as below so above"

Pray (v.) early 13c. The word prayer or prārthanā (in Sanskrit) is derived from two words 'pra' and 'artha' meaning pleading zealously. It is asking for something with intense yearning. (Deep desire) Through a prayer a devotee is sending out a plea. Pray is sending out and mediation is receiving within.

Certainty (n.) c. 1300, "The quality of being reliably true" also "A fact that definitely true or event that is definitely going to take place"

Salvation (n.) c. 1200 "deliverance from wrongful thinking and its consequences"

Heart of men to the heart of Allah – The heart signifies the soul of man and the heart of Allah is the Essence of Allah.

Belief (n.) late 12c."To hold dear, care, desire"

Faith (n.) mid 13c."Truthfulness" From early 14c, Assent of the mind to the truth of a statement for which there is a complete evidence"

Fruition (n.) early 15."The point at which a plan or project is realized"

Deific (adj.) late 15c. "Making divine like nature"

One – "Symbolize a sign of unity"

End Notes

Truth is not in words that you speak; truth is when you hold the life within you. Truth is the only authority in creation of its existence.

The subconscious mind, is that part of the physical brain, which completes the bridge between the physical brain and the spirit. It also collects many things which pass through the conscious brain but which are not retained by it.

Prayer is not an act; it is a certain quality that you bring into your life by which it means that prayer is a positive mental transaction of thought energy form from your conscious to your subconscious, with the intent of sending out those positive thoughts unto yourself within yourself. With that activity and purpose to receive back from the prayer that is being given. Be very mindful from which you are praying for.

CHAPTER VIII

JESUS REVEAL TO THE PEOPLE OF THEIR SINFUL WAYS

ORISSA – Also know as Odisha, is a state in India, located on the east coast of India, by the Bay of Bengal.

Katak - (Cuttack) Means army cantonment (A temporary troop accommodations) and also the capital city. The history of Cuttack amply justifies its name. The city Cuttack stated as a military cantonment because of its impregnable situation that further developed into the capital of the state of Odisha (formerly Orissa)

Jagannath (or Jagannatha) meaning "Lord of the Universe" or "Master of the world" It is a deity worshipped by Hindus and Buddhists mainly in the Indian states in Orissa. Jagannath is considered a form of Vishnu or his avatar Krishna by the Hindus. Jagannath is worshipped as part of triad on the jeweled platform, the icon of Jagannath is a carved and decorated wooden stump with large round eyes with stumps as hands, with the conspicuous absence of legs.

Haul (v.) 1580 "Pull or draw forcibly" To transport, as with cart.

Scores (n.) - "A group or set of twenty or about twenty"

Frenzy (n.) mid -14c. "A state or period of uncontrolled excitement or wild behavior.

Altar (n.) - "An altar is any structure upon which offerings such as sacrifices are made for religious purposes" It was usually a raised platform with a flat surface for offerings to a deity.

Car (n.) c. 1300 "A chariot, carriage, or cart"

Krishna means "Dark blue" in Sanskrit. This is the name of Hindu god believed to be a reincarnation of the god Vishnu. The name Krishna also means "All–attractive" The word 'krish' is the attractive feature of the Lord's existence, and 'na' means spiritual pleasure. When the verb 'krish' is added to the affix 'na' it becomes Krishna, which indicates the Absolute truth. The true nature of blueness comes from his energy because his outa ring of Aura as blue, which signifies all-inclusiveness.

Drunk (ad.) mid 14c."Affected by alcohol to the extant of losing control of one's faculties or behavior

Noise (n.) early 13c."A sound, especially one that is loud or unpleasant or that causes disturbance"

Idol (n.) mid 13c."An image or representation of a god used as an object of worship. Also a person or thing that is greatly admired loved or revered.

Shrine (n.) late 14c. "A place regarded as holy because of its associations with a divinity or a sacred person or relic, typically marked by a building or other construction"

Allah's meeting place is in the heart – Heart is the soul.

Still small voice - The voice of the Spirit speaking within the depths of ones being. The still small voice is not an audible voice. It comes from within as spiritual knowing.

Holy One – "Masculine Energy"

Holy Breath – "Famine Energy"

Mortal eyes - "Physical eyes"

Honor (n.) c. 1200 "High respect; esteem"

Harm (n.) "Physical injury, especially that which is deliberately inflicted"

Assist (v.) early 15c. Help (someone)

Covet (v.) mid 13c. "Desire, lust after"

Countenance (n.) mid- 13c. "A person's face or facial expression"

Sacrifice (n.) late 13c. "An act of slaughtering an animal or person or surrendering a possession as an offering to god or to a divine supernatural figure"

Needless (adj.) - "Of something bad" unnecessary; avoidable.

Waste (v.) c. 1300 "Use or expend carelessly, extravagantly or to no purpose"

Incense (n.) late 13c. "A symbol of prayer with its ancient and primordial in nature incense cerate a positive atmosphere. These spiritual essences radiate from center to circumference, and permeate the whole consciousness." Incense is a substance made from nature producing a sweet smell when burned.

Entranced (v.) 1590s "To throw into a trance," "put in" trance (n.) meaning "to delight."

End Notes

Metaphysical meaning of all the cities in the Moorish Holy Koran

The meaning of city/cities signifies fixed states of consciousness or accumulations of thoughts in the various nerve centers of the body, The presiding or central thought-meaning of a city is found in the significance of its name, combined with that of the man, tribe, country, or nation with which it is mentioned.

CHAPTER IX

JESUS ATTENDS A FEAST IN BEHAR AND HERE HE TAUGHT HUMAN EQUALITY

THIS chapter teaches how to transact with humanity.

Fame (n.) early 13c."The condition of being known or talked about by people, especially on account of notable achievements"

Behar (Heb.) - "On the mount" Behar is a place with a very small population in the province of Bihar India, which is located in the continent/region of Asia. Ancient Bihar, known as Magadha, was the center of power, learning, and culture in India for 1000 years.

Ach – An expression "Oh Lord, Oh Heaven"

Thieve (v.) 1520 One who steals another person's property, especially by secrecy and without using force or violence.

Extortion (n.) c. 1300 "To obtain by force or threats"

Courtesan (n.) early 15c."Prostitute, literally "woman of the court"

Aggrieved (adj.) c. 1300 "Annoyed, furious, resentful, angry, " late 14c, "Oppressed in spirit.

Unbraided (v.) - "Find fault with someone; scold"

Robboni - Word origin of Aramaic, "Master teacher" Used as a Jewish title of respect applied especially to spiritual instructors and learned persons.

Consort (v.) early 15c. "Habitually associate with (someone) , typically with the disapproval of others"

Shun (v.) - "To avoid; desist, abstain: to hide, seek safety by concealment"

Asp (n.) - Poisonous snake, 1520, "An asp, Egyptian viper"

Screen (v.) - "Examine systematically for suitability"

Sake (n.) - "For the purpose of; in the interest of; in order to achieve or preserve"

Reputation (n.) mid-14c. "The beliefs or opinions that are generally held about someone or something"

Worthless (adj.) 1580's "Having no real value or use"

Baubles (n.) early 14c. "Showy trinket or ornament"

Indices (n.) - "Itemize, inventory, record"

Thoughtless (adj.) 1610 "A person or their behavior) not showing consideration for the needs of other people"

Noise (n.) early 13c. "Loud outcry, clamor, shouting, disturbance, uproar, and brawl"

Shallow (adj.) 1580 - Shallow people are described as being vain and focused on physical perception. Their perception of life is based mostly on beauty property, or money. Actually saying the person lacks depth, tending to look at situations superficially. To judge a person based solely on physical appearance is to show little depth of character, or to appear shallow.

Judge (v.) c. 1200 "Examine, appraise, make a diagnosis; c. 1300, "To form an opinion about"

Merit (n.) c. 1200 "Spiritual credit" (for good works, etc.) c. 1300, and "Spiritual reward," from late 14c. As "Condition or conduct that deserves either reward or punishment"

Precious (n.) - "Beloved or dear person or object," 1706, precious (adj.) mid-13c.

"Costly, honorable, of great worth"

Sum (n.) c. 1300 "Amount, total; collection; essential point; summing up, conclusion"

Scorn (v.) c. 1200 "Deprive of honor or ornament, disgrace"

Guilt (n.) early 14c. "Crime, sin, moral defect, failure of duty"

Shrewd (adj.) c. 1300 "Wicked, evil," from shrewe "wicked man" The sense of "Cunning" is first recorded 1510's.

Polished (adj.) late 14c. "Made smooth"

Coat (v.) - Early meaning, "To cover with substance" is from 1753.

Drunkard (n.) 1520 "Participial adjective from drunk "intoxicated"

Covet (v.) mid-13c. "Desire, lust after" or "Passionate desire, eagerness, ambition"

Deceit (n.) c. 1300 "To express the act or manner of deceiving" or "Course by which one deceives" and fraud is an act or series of acts of deceit by which one attempts to benefit himself at the expense of others.

Pure in heart – "Uncontaminated by negative thoughts"

The vile in heart – "A corrupt, wicked; of no value; of inferior and degrading thought without worldly honor or esteem"

Loathing (n.) late 14c. "Disgust, revulsion; hated"

Mockery (n.) early 15c. "Arrogant, sarcastic"

Mock (v.) mid-15c. "To trick, delude, make a fool of, treat with scorn"

Tinseled (n.) - "Showy or superficial attractiveness or glamour"

Weeds – Signified the cares of the world.

Flower – The flower denotes the memory knowledge of truth of growing wise.

Darnel – Cares of the world growing around the seeker after knowledge of truth.

Thistles – Signifies as pain.

Bur – Symbolic meaning of a system that keeps one from knowing the truth by covering all traditions of knowing the truth.

Parable (n.) mid-13c. Parabol, modern from early 14c, "saying or story in which something is expressed in terms of something else, that is used to illustrate a moral or spiritual lesson.

Farmer – A farmer is the guardian of agricultural rites, seeing out the 'old year' and seeing in the 'new' In spiritual terms, this means that the farmer appears as the catalyst of forces of regeneration and salvation, forces that join every beginning to every end.

Fields – Signifies doctrine, and consequently whatever belongs to the doctrine of the faith.

Ripened (v.) 1560s "Developed to the point of readiness and harvester"

Grain – At the spiritual level grain can symbolize the seed of life and to discover the concealed truth.

Blades – Symbolized as the truth.

Stalk – The system that upholds the teachings of the truth.

Wheat – Denotes the things of love and charity.

Barn – A metaphor for the kingdom of heaven. (A state of mind)

Harvester – Represent the gathering together the thoughts and forces for harmonizing and up building purpose.

Saved – Denotes that one has the awareness of the truth.

Shame (n.) - "Feeling of guilt or disgrace; confusion caused by shame; disgrace, dishonor, insult, loss of esteem or reputation"

End Notes

9 in numerology are the unlimited soul expression of all things, of humanity and its law.

CHAPTER X

JESUS SPAKE ON THE UNITY OF ALLAH AND MAN TO THE HINDUS

BENARES – Known as Varanasi, Banaras or Kashi is a city on the banks of Ganges in the Utter Pradesh state of North India. The spiritual capital of India, it is the holiest of the seven sacred cities. In Hinduism and Jainism, and played an important role in the development of Buddhism.

Udraka – A Hindu Priest who taught the mindfulness principles as they apply to human awareness, heath and personal healing. Udraka taught the uses of the waters, plants and earths; of heat and cold; sunshine and shade; light and dark. He said: "The laws of nature are the laws of health, and he who lives according to these laws is never sick"

Scribe (n.) c. 1200 "Professional interpreter of the Jewish law"

Delight (n.) c. 1200 "Please greatly"

Brotherhood – "An established thought in high spiritual consciousness" This thought springs from the understanding that Allah is the one Father and that all men are Brothers. This is also the same in regards to the Sisterhood.

This universal Allah is one, yet He is more than one; all things are one.

Universal (adj.) late 14c. "All encompassing. There is one life force: the creative universal life" This life is eternal and infinite, from everlasting. 7 Universal Law of "Mentalism" This principle embodies the truth that the ALL is Allah. This entity, the All, is pure spirit, which is unknowable and undefinable. But is regarded in the most ancient traditions as a universal, infinite and living mind. This explains the true nature of energy, power, and matter, and how these are subordinate to the mastery of the mind.

Sweet Breath – "Grate life force" The silent movement of the Universal Creator within all. "To advise" properly.

Bound (adj.) mid-14c. "Joined"

Fiber – (n.) late 14c. "Tread like structure in animal bodies" is from c. 1600.

Thrill (v.) early 14c. "To pierce, penetrate by vibrational energy"

From the center to outer bounds of life – "A transformation of energy that carries a vibrational frequency"

Crush (v.) mid-14c. Crash break "To humiliate, demoralize"

Meanest – "Humblest"

Worm (n.) - "Serpent, snake, reptile" The snake denotes crawling, knotted energy.

Shake (n.) 1660s as "Irregular vibration"

Throne – "Divine Truth"

Sword – Sword signifies purification. In Buddhism the sword symbolism deals with discrimination of thought. In this light cut away ignorance.

Tremble – 11c. "Fear"

Sheath – Symbolize the protection of purity within the mind.

The bird sings out – Birds have a predominantly positive meaning. Birds symbolize the power that helps people to speak reflectively and leads them to think out many things in advance before they take action. Birds also represent the higher states of being which symbolize the human soul.

Song – Song can be an expression of happiness or love; Birds songs are often liked to spring, and/or dawn. Bird songs are vibrations of tones; you must feel and absorb the energy that which will connect you to your higherself...to your spiritual source itself.

Unison (n.) 1570, "One sound or same pitch" especially the interval of an octave. The octave sound is a key vibration of advancing the human body to evolve the soul.

Ant – The ant is consistently a symbol of diligence and industriousness. It is known for wisdom, prudence, or foresight. Ant community, discipline, planning, persistence, order, patience, stamina, energy, group minded, teamwork, self and sacrifice.

Bee – The bee is symbolic of fertility, community, prosperity, diligence and work ethic. Some cultures view bees as messengers of the creator. The shape of bee's honeycomb (a hexagon) is similar to a heart, symbolizing the sweetness and love of life that human beings can find in their own hearts. Bee community, organized, industrial, produce, wise, celebration, defensiveness, obsessive nature, and enjoy life.

Spider – The spider is an ancient symbol of mystery, power, and growth, just as the spider weaves a web, so too must weave our own lives. The spider symbol meaning here serves as a reminder that our choices construct our lives.

Flowers – The flowers in its essence are associated with the sun, because the arrangement of its petals is reminiscent of the shape of a star; they may be representatives of spring, with its beauty and the color of the flower often has a great deal to do with the symbolism of its energy it carries.

Deities (n.) c. 1300 the term deity denotes the concepts of sacred or divine.

Kill (v.) c. 1300 "To deprive of life, put to death"

Cruelty (n.) early 13c. "Rude, unfeeling; brutal, hard-hearted"

Awry (adj.) late 14c. "Wrong"

Pain (v.) c. 1300 "To hurt, cause or inflict pain" or "To cause sorrow, grief, or unhappiness"

Lawyer (n.) late 14c. "Lawyer are legal counselors" During this time they were the interpreters of Hindus religious law.

Compressed (v.) c. 1300 "To contain, surround, enclose"

Hedged (v.) late 14c. "Surround with barricade"

Man's idea of god – A mental pattern

Triune Allah – Wisdom, Will, Love – Mind, Sense and Expression.

Brahaman called him Prabrahma – Brahaman means "Greatest" and The belief of Hindu Dharam is that Prabrahma, one supreme Bhagwan, or God is unparalleled and the highest entity.

Egypt He is Thoth – Egypt (GK) Coptic land: from the name Mizraim. Thoth or Djehuti was God of the moon, knowledge, measurement, wisdom, the alphabet, records, thought, intelligence, meditation, the mind, logic, reason, reading, hieroglyphics, magic, scribes and writing.

Zeus is His name in Greek – Zeus the name of the Greek god, related to the old Indo-European god "Dyeus" which meant, "Sky and thunder god" Zeus was identified as Amun or Amun-Ra of Egypt who was the king of the Gods. The noun Greek in ancient meaning of "Cheater"

Jehovah is His Hebrew name – Jehovah which means "He who is, who was, who will be manifest; the self-existent One"

Causeless cause – Causeless (adj.) having no justifying cause or reason"

Cause (n.) c. 1200 "Reason for action, motive"

Rootless Root – Rootless (adj.) late 14c, "Having no settled home or social or family ties" Root- "The basic cause, source, or origin of something"

Grown (adj.) late 14c. "Increased in growth"

Afraid (adj.) early 14c."Impressed with fear, fearful"

Fancy – The adjective is recorded from 1751 in the sense "Fine, elegant, ornamental"

Garbs (n.) 1620s "Clothing or dress, especially of distinctive or special kind"

Priest (n.) Old English probably shortened from the older Germanic form represented by Old Saxon and Old High German prestar. All from Vulgar Latin prester "priest," from Late Latin presbyter "presbyter, elder," from Greek prebyteros.

Restrain (v.) mid-14c. "Prevent (someone or something) from doing something: keep under control or within limits.

Wrath – Wrath was identified here as extreme anger or rage, in which the priests had taught their followers to fear so that they may control individual's emotions to exploit their minds.

Intercede (v.) 1570's "Intervene, come between" or "To interpose on someone's Behalf"

Hand – The metaphysical meaning of hand signifies protection, authority, power and strength.

Strove – Past tense of strive (v.) c. 1200 "Quarrel argue"

Obsessed (adj.) mid-15c. "Tormented" or "Overcome by negative thoughts"

Tarried (v.) early 14c. "To delay, hinder"

Generous soul – One who takes complete responsibility for their own lives. They do not blame others or circumstances for their problems.

Seeker after truth – A seeker is someone who makes sincere efforts to grow spiritually by developing qualities, reducing defects and maintaining a learning attitude.

Abode (n.) mid 13c. "Customary residence"

End Notes

Yeshua sought to learn the Hindu art of healing and became the pupil of Udraka. Udraka was the greatest of the Hindu healers.

"Hindu" is not a Sanskrit word It is not found in any thousands of dialects and languages of India. Neither is a religious word. Hinduism is really not a religion it is only the area in which the people identified with, what is referred to the river as Indus and the land east of the river. Therefore Hindu is a geographic name rather than a demographic or religious name.

THIS BOOK

WITHIN the law of leaning: Accept only that which appeals to your heart as truth, and let the rest pass you by, for the time being- for each comes his own; and none can gain his own, until he is prepared for it.

Front cover signifies that when a book is open you will learn something new. This book is the material incarnation of knowledge and wisdom.

This extraordinary Eso-Science Wordbook Vol. I is a collection of words and phrases for the Moorish Holy Koran. It's contents reveals explanations, definitions from the front cover to chapter 10. Eso- means within and Science is what is known.

In regards to Yeshua (Jesus) to truly understand the lessons of life, you must study just not the human form but rather study the life in such a way that you will learn from the instructions of the lesson of life. "I am the message that I bring to you"

Each chapter holds valuable instructions for one to enter into. These lessons are to be strictly practiced and preserved by the individual. A chapter is like a door that you may enter or close. Enter signifies to study within an open mind so that the individual will evolve for unlimited capacities to progress. Close which indicate a close mind, which there is only a limit for which the individual can obtain.

So, it was said that the Roman numerals originated from seven basic symbols of the Latin alphabet. These symbols I, II, III, IV, V, VI, VII, VIII, IX, X, add up to 10. The Latin alphabet has its roots from the Phoenicians (Canaanites) from the people living in or near Egypt. It was known as hieroglyphics, the Greeks built on the Phoenician alphabet and the rest is history. The Moorish Holy Koran uses the Canaanite symbols for its 48 chapters. Remember that Rome adopted the numerals into their culture.

Al'Kwarizi was an Islamic mathematician who wrote on Hindu-Arabic numerals and was among the first to use zero as a placeholder in positional base notation.

The eventual fall of Roman Empire by 300 A.D. saw the introduction and adoption of Arabic numerals. The reason they are more commonly known as "Arabic numerals" in Europe and the Americas is that they were introduced to Europe in the 10th century by Arabs (Moors) of North Africa, who were then using the digits from Libya to Morocco.

BCE/CE - Usually refers to Common Era (the years are the same as AD/BC). That is, BC is usually understood to mean "Before the Common Era" and CE to mean "Common Era"

C – Circa (from Latin, meaning 'around, about'), "approximately" in several European languages including English, usually in reference to date. Circa is widely used in genealogy and historical writing when the dates of events are not accurately known.

7th century - The 7th century is the period from 601 to 700 in accordance with the Julian calendar in the Common Era. The Moslem conquest began with the unification of Arabia by Mohamet starting in 622.

Abbreviation

(n.) Noun – A word used to identify any of a class of people, places, or things common noun.

(v.) Verb – A word used to describe an action, state, or occurrence, and forming the main part of the predicate of a sentence.

(Adj.) Adjective – A word or phrase naming an attribute, added to or grammatically related to a noun to modify or describe it.

(Pron.) Pronoun – A word or phrase that may be substituted for a noun or noun phrase that has already been mentioned or that already been known, often to avoid repeating the noun.

(Prep.) Preposition – A word governing, and usually preceding, a noun or pronoun and expressing a relation to another word or element in the clause.

(Heb.) Hebrew – A member of ancient people descended from the East, which develops the Semitic language of the Hebrews, in its ancient or modern form. Semitic relating to denoting of languages that includes

Hebrew, Arabic, and Aramaic and certain ancient languages such as Phoenician and Akkadian, constitute the main subgroup of Asiatic family.

Universal Laws

There are seven major Universal Laws by which the entire Universe is governed- Three are immutable. This means they cannot change or be altered in any way. They are absolute, have always existed and will always exist. The other four Laws are transitory, mutable Laws meaning that they can transcended or at least "better used" to create your ideal reality. Your aim is to master each of the seven Universal Laws and only then learn to transcend the mutable ones.

1. Mentalism (Immutable)
2. Correspondence (Immutable)
3. Vibration (Immutable)
4. Polarity (Mutable)
5. Rhythm (Mutable)
6. Cause & Effect (Mutable)
7. Gender (Mutable)apter

www.ingramcontent.com/pod-product-compliance
Lightning Source LLC
Chambersburg PA
CBHW050442010526
44118CB00013B/1645